RAY HAMILTON

summersdale

THE JOY OF CYCLING

Summersdale Publishers Ltd
46 West Street
Chichester
West Sussex
PO19 1RP
UK

www.summersdale.com

Printed and bound by CPI Group (UK) Ltd, Croydon, CRO 4YY

ISBN: 978-1-84953-457-4

Substantial discounts on bulk quantities of Summersdale books are available to corporations, professional associations and other organisations. For details contact Nicky Douglas by telephone: +44 (0) 1243 756902, fax: +44 (0) 1243 786300 or email: nicky@summersdale.com.

Acknowledgements

My thanks to Chris Turton at Summersdale for his unswerving patience and excellent guidance (again), and to Emily Kearns for an extremely thorough job in copy-editing out the wrinkles.

Note from the Author

The websites I have come across in my research for this book are too numerous to list, but I do recommend the first-class British Cycling website (www.britishcycling.org.uk), which I have used extensively to check facts and fill in gaps in my knowledge. It contains a wealth of information about how to get into whatever cycling you want to get into, as well as information about British riders and events across the entire competition range. If your cycling pursuits are purely leisurely, you should also check out the national cycling charity CTC's website (www.ctc.org.uk).

To the best of my knowledge, the facts and figures in this book are correct as at the end of May 2013.

CONTENTS

Introduction..6

Chapter 1 – The 'Eruption' of the Bicycle.............................9

Chapter 2 – The Evolution of Revolution........................15

Chapter 3 – Town and Country......................................32

Chapter 4 – In the Club...46

Chapter 5 – Bike Racing..59

Road...61

Track..84

BMX..91

Mountain Bike...93

Cyclo-cross..95

Cycle Speedway...97

Hall of Fame..98

Chapter 6 – Classic Racing Bikes..................................107

Chapter 7 – In Training...113

Chapter 8 – Looking the Part......................................122

Chapter 9 – Famous Easy Riders.................................126

Chapter 10 – Bigger, Better, Faster, Stranger… 143

Chapter 11 – Cool Again!...157

INTRODUCTION

Bicycling is a healthy… pursuit, with much to recommend it, and, unlike other foolish crazes, it has not died out.
THE DAILY TELEGRAPH, 1877

Cycling has a lot going for it. Speed, for one thing. The ability to travel at around three times the pace of walking for the same amount of effort remains as attractive now to millions of adults and children across the globe as it was to the early riders of the 'boneshakers' and penny-farthings of the late nineteenth century. Cycling also has longevity going for it. Most bike riders start young and many will

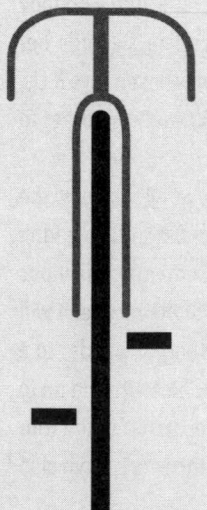

keep riding until well into their twilight years, whether for reasons of health or general fitness, or just for the sheer fun of it. And there are those who could simply not imagine life without the more extreme forms of cycling – from professional racers to round-the-world tourers, from daredevil mountain bikers to Guinness World Record seekers.

Bikes feature in many of our earliest memories. For me, it was trying to keep up with my older brother, Ken, as he pedalled effortlessly for miles over a ridiculous number of hills to the sand dunes of Irvine or the shores of Loch Lomond. There were times on those days when I found it difficult to remember what he looked like from the front!

And we never forget the first time a child of our own pedals away without stabilisers. At first oblivious to the fact we have let go of the saddle, then the inevitable wobble of panic as they realise we are no longer there, then the look of joy/relief/satisfaction on their little faces as they realise they are going to survive! With my daughter, Holly, it was more a look of grim determination. As a child who took her childhood very seriously, she went on to declare Halfords her favourite shop at the age of seven. She could have chosen Toys R Us, but she didn't. She chose a bike retailer. Sometimes it's hard not to be proud of them.

But no childhood memories of, or lifelong love affairs with, the bike would be possible if a volcano in the Dutch East Indies hadn't erupted in 1815. This book will justify that seemingly ridiculous claim before looking at the earliest incarnations of the bicycle. It will then follow the evolution of the bicycle from a thing of wonder to a utilitarian form of transport, to a thing of aesthetic pleasure and on to the lean, mean racing machines that we marvel at during the Tour de France or the Olympics. It will look at the bike's survival in the face of monstrous levels of motorised transport and rejoice in its recent resurgence.

As the human race re-evaluates its position on planet Earth, bikes are once more being seen as an integral part of the future, not the past. On account of their obvious ecological, financial and health advantages, they are once more part of the solution, not the problem. Even that troublesome sub-species of the human race, the politician, has recognised the potential of the bike to solve a number of the world's problems. Some city mayors are already bringing smiles to the faces of cyclists with city-centre rental schemes; with more, safer cycle lanes and paths; and with increased parking for bikes at the expense of cars. Others will follow, either because it's the right thing to do or because it will help them get re-elected. Who cares, as long as they do it?

Like all subject matter of such historical, cultural and practical significance, cycling is awash with interesting characters and anecdotes. This book will delve into them. For example, I once read about a young cyclist who pretended to be a vegetarian to get on the Linda McCartney Racing Team when he was trying desperately to make a name for himself in the sport. Bradley Wiggins, I think his name was. I wonder whatever happened to him?

CHAPTER 1

THE 'ERUPTION' OF THE BICYCLE

Progress should have stopped when man invented the bicycle.
ELIZABETH WEST, *HOVEL IN THE HILLS*

In 1815 the volcanic Mount Tambora in the Dutch East Indies erupted, and it forgot to stop. Within three months, it had filled the skies of the northern hemisphere with grey ash cloud, blocking out the sun and causing northern Europe and North America to be drenched in cold rain. The following year became known as 'the year without a summer'. Crops failed, including the oats needed to feed horses, so farmers and other horse owners had to shoot them rather than let them die of starvation.

It is thought that the resulting lack of horses inspired the German inventor Karl Drais to research new ways of horseless transportation, and led him in 1817 to invent the literally revolutionary all-wooden Laufmaschine (running machine), also known as the Draisine and the 'hobby horse'. There were no pedals but there were two wheels joined together and a means to steer them in a forward motion as your legs ran at a pace hitherto unknown to mankind. This was the ancestor of the modern bicycle and a definite step toward mechanised personal transport. Agriculture recovered, however, and Drais's idea was shelved for the next 40 years or so.

But Drais would not be denied, even if he did have to wait until after his own death for his idea to be taken further! In the second half of the nineteenth century, trial and error spawned a bewildering array of contraptions that followed the basic form of Drais's running machine:

Boneshaker

With pedals now attached to the front wheel, the velocipedes (literally, 'fast feet'), or boneshaker, invented in 1860s Paris did indeed shake the

bones as riders traversed the cobblestones of the city. The pain was eased slightly on these all-wooden bicycles with the later addition of metal 'tyres', but not by much. Only the rich could afford to own one outright, as they are said to have cost the equivalent of an average worker's pay over six months, and not that many people could afford to rent them by the minute even in the rinks that were set up for that purpose in Europe and America.

Not many original boneshakers survive, as most were melted down to help produce the armaments of World War One, and those that do survive command prices of several thousand pounds when they change hands.

Penny-farthing

This was a 'high-wheeler' made from metal in the 1870s and 1880s, and named 'penny-farthing' on account of its different-sized wheels. The rider sat on a saddle over the much larger front wheel, which was so designed in order to better absorb the shock of metal wheels on poorly paved surfaces. This front wheel was up to 1.5 metres (5 feet) in diameter, about double the size of today's bicycle wheels, while the smaller rear wheel was a mere 40 cm (16 in) in diameter.

The penny-farthing became ridiculously popular, given how difficult and dangerous it was to ride. Cycling schools were set up to teach the basic skills required, but problems with braking, steering, or just staying on in a breeze, still took their toll. Injury, and quite often death, awaited those who were suddenly rotated 180 degrees forward after applying the brakes. For obvious reasons, this became known as 'taking a header' – and the penny-farthing came to be referred to as the 'widow-maker'.

When 'safety' bicycles (see below) were introduced in the mid 1880s, diehard penny-farthing riders would come to refer somewhat ironically to their bikes as 'ordinaries' in order to distinguish them from the newfangled contraptions with similar-sized wheels.

Re-cycled Fact

'It's like riding a bike'

We may not easily forget how to ride a bike, but it's not always that easy to get the hang of it in the first place. Nowadays parents can teach their children the skill and balance required, but that wasn't the case for the early riders. It was such an unnatural thing for them to ride a velocipede, never mind a high-wheeler like the penny-farthing, that riding instruction books were published and riding academies, very much the equivalent of today's driving schools, sprang up on both sides of the Atlantic to satisfy the demand.

High-wheel tricycle

While men rotated to death on their own front axles, many ladies who were confined to their corsets and long skirts took to the parks on tricycles with two giant rear wheels and one smaller front one. These machines also afforded greater dignity to gentlemen such as doctors and clergymen, who could not be seen to be flying through the air by the members of Victorian society they served. Queen Victoria herself owned such a high-wheeled tricycle, a 'Royal Salvo', but there is no evidence that she rode it.

High-wheel safety

More of a 'farthing-penny' than a penny-farthing, as the rider-carrying large wheel was swapped to the back in an attempt to reduce the 'death by rotation' statistics. The smaller wheel at the front prevented the whole bike from rotating forwards when the brakes were applied.

Rover safety

The British cycling industry started in Coventry and took a huge step forward with the introduction there of John Starley's 'Rover' in 1885. Now back to two wheels of similar height (so that both feet could be placed 'safely' on the ground), but with solid rubber tyres, a steerable front wheel and a chain drive to the rear wheel, the Rover was much faster than anything that had come before and a bit more comfortable. The riders of high-wheelers literally and metaphorically looked down on these new imposters, referring to them as 'dwarf machines', 'beetles' and 'crawlers'.

But it was during the development of Starley's safety bikes that the diamond-shaped frame that has survived to this day came to be recognised as the most efficient and effective design for the core of a bicycle; and the addition of pneumatic tyres in the 1890s was welcomed by backsides everywhere and continues to be appreciated (or, at least, taken for granted) by the posteriors of today.

Re-cycled Fact

Air we go!

John Dunlop was a Scottish veterinary surgeon practising in Belfast in 1887 when he took it upon himself to develop the first practical pneumatic tyre to make his young son's tricycle more comfortable. Willie Hume, the captain of the Belfast Cruisers Cycling Club, proved the tyre's worth by winning races on it and commercial production began in 1890.

And so it was towards the end of the nineteenth century that the bicycle once more came to threaten the horse as the main form of human transport, but this time without the aid of volcanic eruption or crop failure. As Butch Cassidy (Paul Newman) declared after performing stunts on a 'safety' bike to impress Etta Place (Katharine Ross) in *Butch Cassidy and the Sundance Kid*: 'The future's all yours, you lousy bicycle.'

Ironically, the bicycle industry itself came under threat not too long after its products were popularised by the masses. In a sense, the industry gave itself a flat tyre by inventing the mechanics and pneumatics that would soon be applied to the early forms of the motor car. The Wright brothers would even have the audacity to apply the knowledge they gained repairing bikes to their rudimentary flying machines. And the riders of bikes didn't help either, demanding the improved surfaces that would literally pave the way for the motor car.

But the bike would survive and so, for the record, would the horse, which finds itself in the twenty-first century threatened more by the food chain than the volcano or the bike.

CHAPTER 2

THE EVOLUTION OF REVOLUTION

Other forms of transport grow daily more nightmarish.
Only the bicycle remains pure in heart.

Iris Murdoch, *The Red and the Green*

It is fair to say that the bicycle has been life changing for many people, and for many different reasons. In this chapter we will look at its usage and development in the context of the role it has played (primarily in Britain) in the pursuit of everything from leisure and business, to war and the emancipation of women.

Cultural change

For those who could afford them in the late nineteenth and early twentieth centuries, bicycles made possible day trips, or even whole weekends away. Hitherto unexplored countryside was explored; as yet unseen seasides were seen. For many women, bicycles also meant an end to total reliance on men for transport.

Bicycle trips educated people about the geography and ways of life that existed beyond their natural doorsteps. City boys and girls met country boys and girls, and within a generation the gene pools of an area were extended as far as it was possible to cycle in a weekend. There may even have been some cross-fertilisation across the class divide as social barriers are said to have largely fallen away on bike rides, even if those barriers went straight back up on a Monday morning back in the real world.

The unprecedented social change of the time was personified in a remarkable 16-year-old girl called Tessie Reynolds, who, in 1893, took it into her head to cycle all the way from her home in Brighton to London Bridge and back in a day. This didn't just show that a young woman could be a supreme athlete, it showed that she didn't have to live her whole life in the town or village or street in which she was born.

Clothing was an immediate issue for female bike riders, it being apparent from the start that bicycle pedals could not be operated from the 'ladylike' side-saddle position then employed on a horse. Corsets and petticoats had to stay in the wardrobe if women were to enjoy the freedom and equality promised by the bicycle. Tailors got rich quick by providing the bloomers, knickerbockers and divided skirts that allowed women to mingle unchaperoned with their male counterparts on bicycle rides and to join in unisex games like bicycle polo. At a more utilitarian level, some women would even find the bicycle an indispensable means of carrying out their jobs, particularly those, such as midwifery, that involved getting from house to house over a wide catchment area.

In spite of such heady beginnings for the fairer sex, however, cycling remained largely a male pastime. Initially, this had much to do with the costs involved, and with the fact that the predominantly male family breadwinner had more need for transport than those left at home.

But even in 2013, according to the annual survey commissioned by British Cycling, only about 2 per cent of women in the UK cycle at least once a week, as opposed to 6 per cent of men. British Cycling is trying to encourage women-only cycling events in an attempt to redress the balance, which would suggest that the unchaperoned mingling of the sexes has not turned out to be everything it was cracked up to be in Victorian Britain. (See Chapter 4 for more details about cycling opportunities for men and women.)

On the job

In addition to the midwifery already mentioned, other professions that were to make extensive use of the bike included the following:

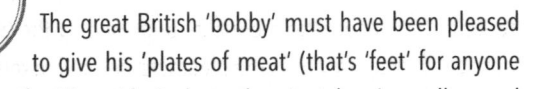

Police officer

The great British 'bobby' must have been pleased to give his 'plates of meat' (that's 'feet' for anyone unfamiliar with Cockney rhyming slang) a well-earned rest upon the advent of the bicycle, and must initially have felt greatly empowered to be on a form of transport quicker than the foot. (Although I do accept that the odd criminal might have escaped over the fields on horseback, I doubt it would have been a very common occurrence.)

Taking a lead from the USA over a hundred years later, a twenty-first-century revival is seeing mobile police officers on state-of-the-art mountain bikes in many of our cities and rural areas. Advantages are considered to be: faster response times compared with police officers on foot or police cars stuck in traffic; rapid access to incidents in places like housing estates, playing fields or canal towpaths; and greater connection with the younger generation – it's easier to impress on something like a Santa Cruz Chameleon Pursuit Pro bike than on the giant, heavy roadsters that were used by police officers in the first half of the twentieth century. Some businesses, including Tesco, McDonald's and the Co-op, are so keen on having their areas patrolled that they have funded the provision of bikes to their neighbourhood police units.

Soldier

As early as the Second Boer War (1899–1902), scouts and messengers used bikes, and cycle-mounted infantry conducted raids on both sides. An army cycling manual of the time recommended that riders should turn their bikes upside down and spin the wheels in order to spook enemy cavalry horses.

In World War One, the Germans had cycling companies within each of their 80 infantry battalions and the British Army had an entire Cyclist Division. In 1937, Japan included around 50,000 bicycle troops when it invaded China. In World War Two, BSA Airborne folding bicycles were parachuted in with the Allied paratroopers that would use them to make a quick getaway as soon as they were on the ground behind enemy lines.

Postal worker

The jolly image of the postman delivering letters on his trusty bike started with the penny-farthing of the late nineteenth century. Although a quarter of the nation's letters were still being delivered on tens of thousands of 'Pashley Red' bicycles as late as the 1970s, most have since been withdrawn and only a few hundred survive in rural areas. The others have fallen victim to road safety concerns.

Butcher's boy

This black classic roadster was designed to carry heavy loads in the large wicker basket over the front wheel, and had a large metal plate hanging from the crossbar to advertise the company colours and logo. As with the Post Office bikes, these 'Delibikes', as they are now known, were mainly made by the Pashley bicycle company that started up in 1926 and is still going strong today.

Factory worker

Memories of factory workers pouring through the gates en masse on their bikes were revived in the 2010 British film, *Made in Dagenham*, which portrayed the struggle of women in 1960s Britain to get the same pay rates as male workers involved in the production of cars. Commuting to work by bike remains hugely popular in some towns and cities around the world, and even in pockets of Britain. (See Chapter 3 for more information.)

Re-cycled Fact

That Hovis ad on the telly

The 'butcher's boy' bike was equally useful for the delivery of bread, as evidenced by the iconic 1973 Hovis ad that forever implanted the theme from Dvorak's New World Symphony into British consciousness. The nation sighed nostalgically as 'Boy on Bike' delivered bread to old Ma Peggity at the top of Gold Hill in Shaftesbury, Dorset, before freewheeling back down to enjoy his own Hovis doorsteps when he got home. The ad was directed by none other than future Alien, Gladiator and Blade Runner *director Ridley Scott.*

The motorised enemy

As soon as Henry Ford launched his Model T car, otherwise known as the 'Tin Lizzie', in 1908, bikes stopped being man's newest toy, but for

another half a century the bike would remain the only toy that most people could afford. As the economic effects of World War Two finally began to wear off in the 1950s and 1960s, more people took to the roads in mechanised forms of transport and the bike was increasingly looked upon as the poor man's car, or the young person's plaything. In some cases, manufacturers even stopped worrying about whether bikes worked. The Raleigh Chopper and its smaller version, the Tomahawk, looked great, but they felt like they were designed for circus clowns to ride round and round on in the big top. However much you wanted to, it was very difficult to run away from home on a bike with 'ape-hanger' handlebars, different-sized wheels and a spongy saddle the size of a small sofa.

As money was ploughed into car manufacturing (Peugeot, Opel, Morris, Rover, Hillman and Humber are just some of the bike manufacturers that converted to car-making) and the road infrastructure needed to support it, cycling became increasingly difficult and dangerous. As we will see, it would be the end of the twentieth century before politicians and planners started to address the folly of the decisions that their predecessors had taken, in terms of the environment and in terms of the health and well-being of the world's citizens.

Cycling remained more popular in western mainland Europe than in other developed countries in the twentieth century, primarily because road racing was a huge sport in countries like France, Italy and Spain. Roads were less crowded in parts of those countries than in Britain, particularly in the mountains where much of the racing took place. (We will take a much closer look at road and other types of racing in Chapter 5.)

Cycling also remained popular in areas like South East Asia and China, where the gulf between the rich and poor encouraged parallel economies – a motorised economy for the rich and a bicycle/rickshaw economy for the poor. As the poor outnumbered the rich, so bicycles continued to outnumber cars in the Orient long after cars had started to force bikes off the roads of western Europe.

In America, off-road cycling and bikes remained especially popular throughout the twentieth century. Initially, this was down to the popularity of track cycling as a spectator sport. Almost every major city had a velodrome in the first half of the twentieth century. The annual races at Madison Square Garden were as popular as baseball and gave rise to the Madison track cycling event that continues to this day. Track cycling did eventually fall behind baseball and American football in the national psyche by the middle of the century, but it would later be replaced by the mountain-bike and BMX crazes that swept the nation from the 1970s onwards.

A bike for everyone!

Bicycles have evolved in different shapes and sizes, using different technologies and materials, in order to meet the demands of a wide range of bike riders across the world:

Mountain bike

Robust and great for off-roading, the mountain bike is ideal for the cross-country enthusiast who prefers woodland mud, rocky paths, tricky climbs and death-defying technical descents.

It was pioneered in 1970s America by the likes of Joe Breeze, Gary Fisher, Charlie Kelly and Tom Ritchey, and was a bit of a cross between a road bike and a BMX. It had heavier tubing than a road bike, and a wider fork to accommodate a wider tyre and bouncier suspension. Gary Fisher's name in particular became synonymous with the mountain bike, but the two first mass-produced models were the magnificently named Specialized Stumpjumper and the Univega Alpina Pro.

The bike industry was initially unimpressed by the upstart mountain-biking fraternity but the latter's passion developed into, and very much remains, a mainstream activity across the globe.

BMX

Strong but light frames and smooth tyres make these the ideal bikes for practising tricks on. Perfect your hops and grinds, and your 180s and 360s, before progressing to BMX racing, the newest Olympic sport of all.

BMX is short for 'bicycle motocross' and the bikes were in fact designed in 1970s California in order to replicate the thrills and spills of the popular motocross sport for youngsters. The size and availability of chopper-style bikes like the Schwinn Sting-Ray made them the only natural choice for BMX racing at the time, and the basic design that remains today stemmed from that style. Notwithstanding the lack of grip on the smooth tyres of a BMX bike, brakes are not considered necessary – apparently that's what feet are for.

Other bikes styled on the chopper motorbikes rendered iconic by the 1969 American road movie *Easy Rider*, and customised for BMX racing in the 1970s, included the then ubiquitous Raleigh Chopper and Tomahawk, also referred to as 'wheelies' (most of the weight was on the back, so doing a 'wheelie' was easy), 'high-risers' (on account of the 'ape-hanger' handlebars) and 'banana bikes' (on account of the curved saddle).

Racing

Light and fast for those who take their cycling seriously, racing bikes are ideal for long-distance commuting, club cycling and, of course, professional road racing. Variations include triathlon and time-trial (TT) bikes.

The early steel monsters ridden by the European road racers of the late nineteenth century have continually evolved into today's lightweight machines incorporating state-of-the-art aerodynamics and electronic componentry. (We will look more closely at that evolution, and at some iconic racing bikes, in Chapter 6.)

Hybrid

A hybrid is lighter than a mountain bike but sturdier than a racer, so is a great crossover option for cycling around towns and cities, as well as the countryside. It will also cope with 'mild' off-roading.

Size and riding position are influenced by the mountain bike (for example, a hybrid has flat handlebars), but the smoother tyres are akin to those of racing bikes and make for better rolling on paved, or at least smooth, surfaces. Many manufacturers produce different variations on the hybrid theme, and you will see them advertised also as 'town and city', 'comfort', 'multi-use', 'lifestyle', 'commute', 'urban', 'fitness' and whatever else takes the marketing department's fancy. They are often designed with facilities like luggage racks (so they're not unlike touring bikes in that respect), as well as clothes-protecting mudguards and enclosed chain guards.

It is difficult to say when the first hybrids were introduced to the market as they have largely morphed from existing bike designs over the past two or three decades. The mass manufacturers today include Specialized and Giant.

Touring

This bike does what it says on the tin and is designed for comfort over long distances, with sufficient strength and mounting points to carry heavy luggage. The tandem is a romantic variation if you manage not to fall out for the entire holiday.

It often looks like a normal racing bike from a distance (especially those with dropped handlebars), but closer inspection will reveal a longer-then-usual wheelbase, heavy-duty wheels and the required luggage-mounting points. Touring bikes have been around for as long as people have wanted to tour on bikes, which is a long time. Distance is generally not an object, but if you want to cycle round the world on sometimes-difficult surfaces and/or in sometimes-extreme weather, you would do well to take the advice of trekking specialists to determine just how industrial you need your touring or trekking bike to be. Significant touring bike manufacturers today include Raleigh, Ridgeback and Dawes.

Track

Track bikes are minimalist affairs, designed for speed in a velodrome and nothing else. There are no brakes, no gears and no freewheel – if the back wheel is turning, so are the pedals.

These bikes resemble stripped-down road-racing bikes, and there's not much point in buying one if you don't want to race competitively in a wooden velodrome. There are no hills to negotiate and there is no need to stop or slow down suddenly in a velodrome, hence the absence of gears and brakes.

Roadster

Here is a classic utility bicycle once popular worldwide, not least because Raleigh and BSA exported them throughout the British Empire for as long as that empire held strong, and still very common in Africa, Asia, Denmark and the Netherlands.

A heavy steel but extremely reliable bike, the roadster is easily identifiable by its large wheels and high 'sit-up-and-beg' handlebars. Once ubiquitous in Amsterdam and Beijing, it is still mass-produced in Asia primarily for the sub-Saharan African market. A top-end range is still produced by Pashley Cycles, the British company that produced them for the postal workers, police officers and butcher boys of yesteryear.

Folding

The (normally) small-wheeled utilitarian option, a folding bike saves storage space at home or in the office and can be taken on most forms of public transport. Just don't expect speed from the small-wheeled versions.

Although the folding bicycle is particularly useful nowadays for commuters, it was originally designed to be used by infantry soldiers in the late nineteenth century. The Pedersen folding bicycle was used by the British Army in the Second Boer War, so infantrymen could fold them up and carry them on their backs across terrain that was not suitable for cycling.

Top manufacturers of folding bikes nowadays include Ridgeway, Dahon and Brompton.

Recumbent

This bike places the rider in a laid-back reclining position, with body weight distributed more evenly, and therefore more comfortably, than on a conventional bike. This can be particularly useful for riders with chronic back or neck problems.

Other advantages of the recumbent include increased peripheral vision (because the head is not bent forward), less far to fall in the event of an accident, and improved aerodynamics (a recumbent holds the world speed record for a bicycle). Although it is one of the few types of bike not to adhere to the basic diamond-shaped frame that has been used for bicycles since the late nineteenth century, and although people continue to stop and stare at one as if it has just arrived from outer space, the recumbent has in fact itself been around since the 1800s, having evolved during the early stages of experimental design.

Recumbents are available as bicycles or tricycles (main manufacturers include Optima and Lightning), and as static exercise bikes.

Electric

Also known as an e-bike, you pedal and use the gears as normal but a battery-driven electric motor will do the hard work for you. This is a more expensive option, but great value for money if you use it as an affordable alternative method of mechanised transport (no licence, MOT or petrol needed).

Bikes on film

Bicycles have featured in countless movies and
TV programmes over the years, and not just as
props. From cameo appearances to starring roles,
and sometimes even as the subject of the film
itself, here are my top ten classic bike moments
captured for your viewing pleasure:

1. *The Wizard of Oz (1939)*

The scene where the evil Miss Almira Gulch rides her classic step-
through roadster away from the farm with Dorothy's pet dog, Toto,
in the basket had audiences everywhere screaming 'monster!'.
The frightening music from that scene remains alive and well
today as a popular mobile phone ringtone.

2. *Ladri di Biciclette (Bicycle Thieves) (1948)*

Consistently lauded as one of the great films of world cinema,
it follows the plight of a father in post-war Italy as he struggles to
recover his stolen bike, without which he cannot get the work he
needs to feed his family. Bike scenes abound but we are denied a
happy ending, as the stolen bike in question is never recovered.

3. *The Sound of Music (1965)*

'Do-Re-Mi' on a bike! Well, on eight bikes, actually. Does cinema get more iconic than a Rodgers and Hammerstein classic being belted out by Julie Andrews and seven Alpine children on roadsters?

4. *Butch Cassidy and the Sundance Kid (1969)*

Who could forget that idyllic bike scene as the boys took some time out on a farm in between robberies? The bowler-hatted Butch (Paul Newman) took Etta Place (Katharine Ross) for a spin on the handlebars of his 'safety' bike as B. J. Thomas sang 'Raindrops Keep Fallin' on My Head' to complete the perfect movie moment.

5. *A Day Out (1972)*

Playwright and keen cyclist Alan Bennett's first televised play was this half-hour short film about a Yorkshire cycling club on their outing from Halifax to Fountains Abbey in the summer of 1911. Studley Royal and Ripon are among the locations as we are transported back to simpler times. The tandem crash actually happened and filming had to be edited around the ensuing hospital visit for the two cast members involved.

6. *Breaking Away (1979)*

Winner of an Oscar, a Golden Globe and a BAFTA, this coming-of-age comedy drama about four American college graduates revolves around the passion one of them has for road racing. There are some great racing scenes when a professional Italian road-racing team comes to town, and during the recreation of the Little 500, an annual bike race held at Indiana University.

7. *E.T. the Extra-Terrestrial (1982)*

BMX bikes hadn't existed for long when they landed their first starring film role – and what a role it was. In the 1982 Spielberg classic, the cute extra-terrestrial took his young friend Elliott flying across the night sky, and the flying BMX against the full moon remains one of the most iconic images in movie history.

8. *BMX Bandits (1983)*

Nicole Kidman starred as the crime-fighting, BMX-riding teenager in the Australian children's adventure film *BMX Bandits*. Right from the opening scenes alongside the waterfronts of Manly, and later against the backdrop of Sydney, the film highlights time and again the off-road versatility of the BMX at a time when the BMX craze was sweeping the planet.

9. *Fight Club (1999)*

There is a scene in *Fight Club* where Tyler Durden (Brad Pitt) is cycling through the rooms of the house the two main protagonists share and goes head first over the handlebars. This first happened as an accident when the cameras weren't rolling but the crew and actors found it so funny that they then recreated it for the film. The first rule of Cycling Club is that you have to watch where you're going, Brad.

10. *Transporter 3 (2008)*

The Best Use of a BMX Ever Award must surely go to Frank Martin (Jason Statham) in the third instalment of the French car-action trilogy. Having been carjacked while taking a phone call, he commandeers the nearest form of transport (a BMX bike) and sets off in hot pursuit. Having caught up with the top-of-the-range Audi on the 'borrowed' BMX (of course he does), Frank then does what Frank does best – feet first through the car window, he boots the carjacker straight out the passenger-side door while he himself lands safely in his usual driving-seat position. Perhaps even cooler than flying past the moon with an alien in your front basket? You decide.

CHAPTER 3

TOWN AND COUNTRY

It is by riding a bicycle that you learn the contours of a
country best, since you have to sweat up the hills and coast
down them. Thus you remember them as they actually are,
while in a motor car only a high hill impresses you…

ERNEST HEMINGWAY, AMERICAN AUTHOR AND JOURNALIST

Today, a lot of exciting things are happening to the world's cycling environment. From large-scale urban redevelopment to idyllic rural and waterside cycle paths, planners and developers around the globe are responding to the growing demand for a better, safer cycling infrastructure. The benefits are obvious: healthier living, cleaner environments and more affordable transport.

At the turn of the twenty-first century many politicians and urban planners seemed to wake up to the stupidity of their predecessors, and reports of common sense have been flooding in from around the world ever since.

UK towns and cities

Some UK towns and cities would sit better in the Netherlands or Denmark when it comes to cycling take-up. Around 20 per cent of journeys in York and around 30 per cent of journeys in Cambridge are made on bikes, which is not far off the national averages of our northern European neighbours.

Of course, university towns have always been way more cycle-friendly than larger urban sprawls, not least because most students could afford bikes and not cars. And because these towns already had a cycling infrastructure of sorts (albeit one that had existed for centuries in some cases), they were better equipped to survive the short-sighted movement in the second half of the twentieth century to plan for ever-increasing traffic at the expense of cycling and the environment generally.

In 2005 an investment scheme was launched in the UK to fund safety measures and infrastructure changes that would encourage more people to cycle more often. The scheme included schools-based and business-based education about the benefits of cycling, and 'bikeability' training for children and 'rusty' adults.

Bristol was awarded the status of 'Cycling City' when it launched the UK's first on-street bike-rental scheme in 2008, based on an existing Paris model. London continues to introduce cycle superhighways to aid commuting in and out of the city; safe bike zones that offer traffic-free school runs; and its own bike-rental scheme (run by Montreal-based BIXI).

Out in the country

Away from the cities, more and more cycle paths have been created along the sides of canals and rivers, through national parks, and on top of railway lines abandoned by the short-sighted politics of the 1960s (when, for example, the infamous Beeching report heralded the closure of half of the UK's stations and a third of its tracks in favour of increased road transport). Here is a short selection of some of the UK's most scenic bike rides, plus one foray into France. Some of the rides are not at all taxing; others are not for the fainthearted:

Tudor Trail, Kent

Route: Tonbridge Castle via Penshurst Place to Hever Castle

Distance: 16 km (10 miles)

Time to allow: 2 hours

What to expect: Pretty much traffic-free once you leave Tonbridge, a mixture of off-road (country park), woodland trail and country lanes.

What you see: Haysden Country Park, including Barden Lake; River Medway; Penshurst Place estate; villages of Penshurst, Chiddingstone and Hever; Hever Castle.

Kennet and Avon Canal, Somerset

Route: Bath to Reading

Distance: 136 km (85 miles)

Time to allow: 2–3 days

What to expect: Easy to moderate cycling along towpaths, country lanes and cycle paths.

What you see: Bath; canal locks (including a flight of 16 at Caen Hill); houseboats; aqueducts at Dundas and Avoncliff; the market town of Devizes; north Wessex Downs; southern tip of the Cotswolds.

C2C, Lake District and Pennines

Route: Workington, Whitehaven or St Bees to Tynemouth or Sunderland

Distance: 224 km (140 miles)

Time to allow: 3–5 days (can be done in 1–2 days if you're hard enough)

What to expect: Tough cycling, especially across the Pennines – even tougher if you want to travel east to west into the prevailing wind. Surfaces include minor roads, disused railway lines and specially constructed off-road tracks.

What you see: Irish Sea (off Cumbrian coast); lakes; Castlerigg stone circle; heather moors; Greystoke Castle (home of 'Tarzan'); rugged mountains; the highest café in England; North Sea (off Northumberland coast).

West Country Way

Route: Padstow Harbour to Bath or Bristol

Distance: 384 km (240 miles)

Time to allow: 7–9 days

What to expect: Mixture of roads, cycle paths, towpath and woodland; moderately to very hilly at times.

What you see: Camel Estuary; British Cycling Museum (near Camelford); Bodmin Moor; Exmoor; Somerset Levels; Glastonbury; Wells; Mendip Hills; Bath or Bristol; canals; sea views.

Round the Island Cycle Route, Isle of Wight

Route: East Cowes to East Cowes

Distance: 99 km (62 miles)

Time to allow: 2–3 days (1 day if you're in a hurry and relatively fit)

What to expect: Mostly flat with moderate climbing on cycle paths, country lanes and through towns and villages.

What you see: Cowes; yachts; sea views; Freshwater Bay; the Needles; pretty villages.

Causeway Coast, Northern Ireland

Route: Ballycastle to Giant's Causeway to Ballycastle (circular)

Distance: 56 km (35 miles)

Time to allow: A leisurely few hours to take in the sights.

What to expect: Coastal roads on the way to the Giant's Causeway, hill roads on the way back to Ballycastle.

What you see: Ballycastle; Kinbane Castle; Carrick-a-Rede rope bridge; Ballintoy Harbour; Whitepark Bay; Dunseverick Castle; Giant's Causeway; the Old Bushmills Distillery; Bushfoot Golf Club.

Aviemore to Braemar, Scottish Highlands

Route: Aviemore to Braemar

Distance: 80 km (50 miles)

Time to allow: 1–2 days

What to expect: A road route through the Cairngorms National Park, which, as you might expect, is more than a wee bit hilly in places.

What you see: Aviemore village; the stunning scenery of the Scottish Highlands, including Ben Macdui, the second-highest mountain in the UK; heather moors; Glenlivet and Tomintoul whisky distilleries; Grantown-on-Spey village; Braemar village; Balmoral Castle.

North Wales Cycle Path

Route: Holyhead to Chester

Distance: 173 km (108 miles)

Time to allow: 2–3 days

What to expect: Everything from roads to quiet lanes, towpaths, sea promenades and old railway lines. A 3-mile section around Colwyn Bay is traffic-free. Mostly flat, but can get very windy, especially if you travel east to west into the prevailing wind.

What you see: Isle of Anglesey; Menai Strait; Snowdonia; seaside towns; beautiful coastline; sweeping views over Colwyn Bay; city of Chester.

St Malo, Brittany

Route: St Malo–Dinan–Rennes–Fougères–Mont-Saint-Michel–St Malo (circular)

Distance: 304 km (190 miles)

Time to allow: 4–6 days

What to expect: Relatively flat, some rolling countryside. Includes three separate long-distance traffic-free cycle paths, one following a river then a canal, one on disused railway lines, one on dykes across marshland.

What you see: Harbour town of St Malo; walled citadels; medieval châteaux; charming towns; coastal windmills; the World Heritage Site of Mont-Saint-Michel.

Note: These selections are not intended as route planners, so be sure to check relevant websites (for example, www.sustrans.org.uk) and maps before setting off!

Around the world

Elsewhere in the world there are also some big things happening in bicycle land, and most of them are positively encouraging (but I'm going to have to make an exception when it comes to Beijing):

Amsterdam, the Netherlands

One of the places you would expect things to be happening on bikes, of course. Without over half a million bicycles in its concentrated city centre, Amsterdam would not be Amsterdam. It's a cultural thing as much as anything else, and it's a known fact that all Amsterdammers were in fact born on their bikes.

With almost 500 km (310 miles) of cycle paths, more and more roads being closed to traffic and car parking charges becoming increasingly exorbitant, it is estimated that over 60 per cent of all journeys in the inner city are now made by bike. The classic sturdy Dutch roadsters still in common use throughout the city are the *opafiet* ('grandpa's bike') and *omafiet* ('grandma's bike'). In common with their nineteenth-century ancestors, many of them have no brakes so you have to pedal backwards to slow down or stop.

Portland, Oregon, USA

Portland (population approx. 600,000) has achieved a 10 per cent cycling commuter rate by creating over 420 km (260 miles) of cycle paths to connect its many urban neighbourhoods, and by offering low-cost bicycles, complete with helmet, pump, lock, maps and rain gear, to its less wealthy residents. This take-up rate may not seem high when compared to, say, Amsterdam, but it is more than ten times the American national average and a staggering achievement in the otherwise car-centric Pacific Northwest region. Some companies even reward employees who cycle to work with vouchers that can be spent in the staff canteen.

Re-cycled Fact

Black Mambas

The Chinese industrial invasion of sub-Saharan Africa in recent decades has included the supply of a great many Flying Pigeons (see next page) to Kenya, where they have been re-dubbed 'Black Mambas'. Many have an additional pillion (or passenger) saddle over the back wheel to allow their use as boda-bodas (taxis) and it is not unusual to see a Kenyan mother side-saddling on this two-wheel taxi complete with two or three children.

Beijing, China

There are nine million bicycles in Beijing, as singer-songwriter Katie Melua reminded us in her top-five UK hit of 2005. It is a sad fact, however, that the 'improved' road infrastructure put in place for the 2008 Beijing Olympics brought with it a huge increase in road traffic and made cycling more difficult and more dangerous. City planners now claim to be clawing back the previous position by restoring cycle lanes and introducing bike schemes, but they have a real mountain to climb.

The nine million bikes in question are mostly the roadsters that have been dubbed 'Flying Pigeons', which the revolutionary People's Republic of China decreed to be the approved form of transport for the masses in 1950. This heavy bike, which came in black or black, was considered to be one of three must-haves for each and every citizen, the others being a sewing machine and a watch. It was the perfect symbol of the egalitarian social system of the time – the promise of little comfort but a reliable ride through life. The Chinese government estimates that there are over half a billion Flying Pigeons around China today, many of them handed down from generation to generation.

Copenhagen, Denmark

More than a third of Copenhageners commute to work by bike, making use of around 1,000 km (620 miles) of cycle lanes in the greater Copenhagen area. It is possible to cycle to Roskilde, 30 km (18.75 miles) west of the city, and never leave a bike lane. Cyclists even have their own traffic lights, which let them go before cars.

The bike is like a fifth limb to the residents of Copenhagen, where cycling is a way of life, as opposed to some sort of subculture, which is how it is still viewed by many people in Britain and America. As Danish journalist Mikael Colville-Andersen, the man who coined the term 'cycle chic' to describe how fashionable and comfortable Copenhageners look riding their bikes in everyday clothing, puts it: 'Copenhageners cycle to live, but they don't live to cycle.'

Copenhagen City Bikes, launched in 1995, was the first organised large-scale, urban bike-sharing scheme in the world. The scheme was tragically shelved at the end of 2012 through lack of sponsorship, although not before it had served as a model for the many self-service systems with fixed stands and specially designed bikes that we see around the world today.

Montreal, Canada

Montreal introduced the first self-service urban bike-sharing infrastructure in North America, with over 560 km (350 miles) of cycle paths. Many of the downtown lanes are separated from car lanes by substantial concrete kerbs and the city has become so bicycle-friendly that there have been complaints in winter from motorists about snow being cleared from cycle lanes first. The Montreal scheme, known as the BIXI programme, proved so successful that it has since been rolled out in London, Melbourne, Minneapolis and Washington. The city's greater metropolitan area also boasts a staggering 3,840 km (2,400 miles) of cycle trails, with plans to expand even further.

Paris, France

The Vélib' scheme in Paris was one of the first mass-participation bike-rental systems anywhere in the world, and remains one of the biggest, with around 18,000 bikes and well over a thousand stations covering the city. Vélib' is a portmanteau of the French for bike (*vélo*) and freedom (*liberté*). The operators are working hard to address the two main problems of the scheme: the number of bikes that are stolen (they seem to turn up a lot in Eastern Europe and North Africa); and the problem with bike distribution in the hillier parts of the city – nobody wants to cycle up to Montmartre, but everybody wants to cycle back down.

 Bogota, Colombia

With less than 15 per cent of residents able to afford cars, bikes are something of a necessity to get around a city like Bogota, Colombia, whether it's safe or not. A culture of disrespect for traffic laws and the safety of cyclists still prevails among the city's drivers, resulting in the deaths of hundreds of cyclists each year, so the introduction of safe cycle lanes is as important here as it is anywhere. The city council has already provided over 350 km (219 miles) of cycle lanes, with plans for many more. When certain roads are closed to cars each Sunday around one million residents turn out to enjoy the weekly freedom of safe riding.

Groningen, the Netherlands

There is a definite trend in European cities in particular to increase the number of journeys that are made by bicycle. Basel, Barcelona, Delft and Münster, to name but a few, have all made giant strides. But no city in the world, not even Amsterdam, comes close to the university city of Groningen in the very far north of the Netherlands. Since digging up a six-lane motorway intersection in the city centre in 1977 and replacing it with greenery, pedestrianisation, cycleways and bus lanes, it has achieved a journey-by-bike rate of 57 per cent. Much to the surprise of its many detractors at the time, it also resulted in an economic recovery for the city, as cyclists and bus users returned to city-centre shops and restaurants that they could previously get nowhere near in their cars.

Re-cycled Fact

O sole mio!

The award for Most Brilliant Bike Scheme Initiative in the World Ever must surely go to Trondheim, Norway, for the Trampe, the contraption that takes cyclists up one of its steepest hills. While still sitting on their bikes, riders place the sole of their right foot against one of the moving blocks in a 'tramline' at the edge of the pavement, whereupon the block propels the right foot and everything attached to it to the top of the 1:5 gradient at a speed of 6.4 km/h (4 mph).

CHAPTER 4

IN THE CLUB

Riding a bike is everything to a cyclist. The friendship and camaraderie you have with other cyclists is the be-all and end-all of your life.

TOMMY GODWIN, DOUBLE BRONZE-MEDAL WINNER AT THE 1948 LONDON OLYMPICS

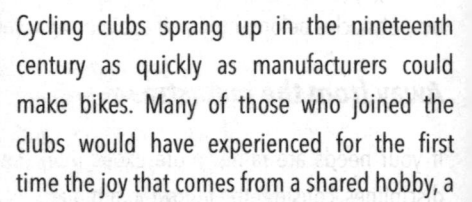

Cycling clubs

Cycling clubs sprang up in the nineteenth century as quickly as manufacturers could make bikes. Many of those who joined the clubs would have experienced for the first time the joy that comes from a shared hobby, a camaraderie that was often less class-ridden than that of other clubs of the day, and a feeling of safety in numbers (it was not uncommon for early bike riders to have insults or even stones thrown at them by those who couldn't or didn't want to join in the fun).

Cycling clubs really took off in a big way with the arrival of penny-farthings in the 1870s and it must have been a sight to behold when hundreds of them rolled along together into the countryside at weekends.

Women were not excluded from the early cycling clubs, although they did sometimes find themselves barred from the social side of things. It was 1922 before the first women-only club was established in the UK, in Rosslyn, and 1956 before the Women's Cycle Racing Association was formed.

Many clubs were set up for the benefit of specific sectors of society, like civil servants, ex-servicemen, card-holding communists or a particular religion. Many had self-evident names, like the Brent Jewish Road Club, the Vegetarian Cycling and Athletic Club, the Theatrical United Cycling Club and the more recently formed No. 1 Muslim Ladies' Cycling Club in east London.

Nowadays, of course, there are clubs for more than just road cycling. There are those that cater specifically for (a combination of) road, track or off-road pursuits, or for the increasingly popular sport of triathlon, which includes cycling along with running and swimming. Perhaps you fancy having a go at cycle speedway, the format of which is pretty much the same as the motorised version, or cyclo-cross, a gruelling cross-country affair which involves you having to dismount to carry your bike over obstacles before setting off again on two wheels.

Away from the mainstream

If your needs are rather more exotic than the mainstream cycling disciplines, consider the following options:

Bicycle polo

Bicycle polo clubs and leagues are springing up around the world. It was traditionally played on grass and looked like it was taking off when it was chosen as a sport for the London 1908 Olympics, but it never really did – until now. The modern hard-court version (indoor and outdoor) has caused a real spike in interest in countries as far apart as Britain, Malaysia, the USA, Australia, Nepal, Brazil and Cuba.

The right club for you

There are clubs that are set up to promote competitive racing in all cycling disciplines, often as potential stepping stones to professional circuits. Check out the British Cycling website to find the Go-Ride club that provides the type of racing you want to get involved in. You will also find information there about the various disability cycling disciplines that exist.

And there are clubs that exist solely to facilitate safe, leisurely cycling for families or children. Check out the CTC (Cyclists' Touring Club) website to find out which clubs might best suit your own needs, including information about all-ability cycling and adapted forms of bicycles.

Tandem riding

Tandem clubs exist for like-minded duos, from those who want to ride for fun in the country to those who want to do some serious touring. Membership will offer opportunities to attend events and rallies, and provide valuable advice on the practicalities of tandeming. Find out what it takes to be the captain on board, or whether you are more suited to the position of rear admiral (yes, it has its own terminology).

Tricycling

Don't be fooled, we're talking about a full programme of events for grown-ups here, at home and abroad, including regular competitions. The first point of contact in the UK is the Tricycle Association, formed in 1928 and still catering today for riders of modern and classic tricycles, and the clubs they belong to.

Veteran cycling

The Veteran-Cycle Club was formed in 1955 and today has worldwide membership of over 2,500, with many special-interest groups depending on the types of cycles and/or marques that members are particularly enthusiastic about. Keeping the past alive for owners and riders of everything from dandy-chargers and penny-farthings to folding bikes and Choppers, local, national and international events are a sight to behold.

The Folding Society

Fancy rolling your Brompton M Type down to the Milton Keynes Origami and chilling out with fellow origamists who may have sneaked in on an Airnimal Chameleon or flown in on a Birdy? If you have answered 'yes', you need to join the Folding Society, which is for all those with an interest in folding bicycles. You can of course travel to any of the Origami Rides by car or train and simply unfold when you get there.

The British Human Power Club

This club organises events and competitions for leg-powered or arm-powered two, three and four-wheeled cycles. Go the whole hog and build yourself a full fairing (any structure added to a vehicle to improve streamlining is a 'fairing') that's as close to a Bluebird as you can get. Recumbent bikes are especially popular in the human-power world, because low-profile plus fairing equals speed!

Bombay Bicycle Club

OK, they're actually an indie rock band from London, but they're better than good so check them out for your on-bike playlist!

Two wheels, too easy?

If even two wheels seem like one too many to you, perhaps you should think about taking up a unicycling activity or sport. Touring unicycles are available if you want to go round the world on one, or, if you would prefer to join the circus or perform at London's Covent Garden, you might want to try out a giraffe (with the saddle up to 3 metres – 10 feet – high), a kangaroo (both feet move in the same parallel direction), or a freestyle (with or without juggling clubs).

But if you would prefer to join a club and take part in an individual or team sport, there are a number of options there as well. The International Unicycling Federation sets the rules for a number of one-wheeled sports, including:

Track events

These range from 100 metres to marathon distance, plus slalom, high jump and long jump. But if you find these a bit easy-peasy, try one of these speciality events:

- The 30 metres walk the wheel (you have to push the tyre with your feet as opposed to using the pedals).
- The 50 metres one-foot (you're allowed to use both pedals for the first 5 metres, but then your foot of choice is on its own all the way to the finish line).
- The slow backward (what it says).

Mountain unicycling (MUni)

Mountain unicycling is an adventure sport that includes cross-country, uphill and downhill. You won't be surprised to learn that you need a strong core and better-than-average balance to be good at any of these disciplines!

Artistic unicycling

Artistic unicycling consists of freestyle events (not dissimilar in format to ice figure skating) for individuals, pairs, groups of three to eight and groups of over eight contestants (a group of 20 is not uncommon). Unicyclists execute their routines, including synchronised moves in the case of groups, to preselected music.

Re-cycled Fact

One-wheeled wonder

The Canadian godfather of off-road unicycling, Kris Holm was the founder and former world champion of unicycle trials (obstacle riding), and he has unicycled to the summits of volcanoes and mountains around the world. Strong leg muscles, do you think?

Unicycle hockey

Using ice hockey sticks and a ball, unicycle hockey is played as far afield as Australia, Korea and Sweden, and there are competitive leagues in the UK, Germany and Switzerland.

Unicycle basketball

This is exactly what you would expect it to be and probably every bit as much fun as it looks. The sport is unsurprisingly popular in the USA and Canada, but the Puerto Rico All Stars has been one of the most dominant teams in the world.

Unicycle Union

If you live in the UK, check out the Union of UK Unicyclists website (www.unicycle.org.uk) for information about clubs in your area, and, just in case you're thinking that unicycling is just for the geeks of the cycling world, check out Chapter 9 for a surprising list of famous unicyclists.

Events and festivals

One of the many advantages of belonging to a cycling club is it opens up access to special (mostly road) events – but you don't have to belong to a club to participate in many of these, or in the growing number of cycling festivals that are springing up. Here is a selection to whet your appetite:

One-day 'classics'

London-Brighton

This annual 86-km (54-mile) charity race on behalf of the British Heart Foundation attracts around 30,000 riders. There is also a 96-km (60-mile) night-time version for insomniacs and a 120-km (75-mile) off-road version for mountain-bike riders.

London to Paris

Join more than a hundred like-minded cyclists to ride just over 500 km (300 miles) from a chosen London location to the Eiffel Tower and raise money for the charity of your choice. After four days of riding to the French capital, the return journey is by Eurostar.

Tweed Run

This annual group bike ride has spread to dozens of cities in every paved continent of the world. UK cities include London and Birmingham, and riders dress in period costume (preferably tweed 'plus fours') to ride (preferably vintage) bicycles and invoke memories of a bygone age.

World Naked Bike Ride

Held annually in 70 cities in 20 countries worldwide, Brighton, York and London are among the UK's participating cities. Other cities include Melbourne, Cape Town and San Francisco, and Portland, Oregon, in the Pacific Northwest of the USA, claims to have the most participants (up to 10,000). The general idea is to remind the world that it has become too oil and car-dependent, and to stress to the world's motorists in particular that cyclists are made of vulnerable flesh and bone. If you don't want to go the whole hog, body paint and/or underpants can be used to disguise your really naughty bits.

Dunwich Dynamo

This overnight ride of 192 km (120 miles) stretches from Hackney in east London to Dunwich on the Suffolk coast. Its popularity is leading to similar through-the-night rides elsewhere, including the Exmouth Exodus (from Bristol) and the night-time London-Brighton run mentioned above.

Pedal for Scotland

This 176-km (110-mile) challenge sees riders make their way from Glasgow to the Scottish capital, Edinburgh. A sportive (this just means 'non-competitive') runs at the same time, but on a parallel route to allow the challenge riders a free rein.

Breeze Bike Rides

A British Cycling initiative to get more women riding and taking part in mass-participation events such as Sky Ride City and Sky Ride Local, and in women-only events like the Cycletta events, a series of challenging but achievable sportives in aid of Macmillan Cancer Support. Championed by Olympic gold medallist Victoria Pendleton, all of these events are suitable for riders of all abilities.

Wiggle Dragon Ride

This prestigious annual Welsh sportive leaves from Margam Country Park, Port Talbot. There are two distances: the Gran Fondo at 216 km (135 miles), which takes in the Brecon Beacons; and the Medio Fondo at 128 km (80 miles). Also includes a women-only Cycletta event.

RideLondon!

Previously known as the London Sky Ride, this showcase cycling festival was rebranded and seriously upgraded for 2013. The equivalent of the London Marathon for cyclists, with Olympic-style road racing thrown in, the format runs something like this:

- A 160-km (100-mile) one-day London-to-Surrey 'classic', featuring many of the world's top male professional riders, including Olympians and well-known Tour de France riders. Starts in the Olympic Park and finishes in the Mall.
- A mass-participation charity-based event, along the lines of the London Marathon, over virtually the same 161-km (100-mile) 'classic' course.
- A professional women's 'criterium' (which is a fixed number of laps around a short road circuit), again featuring many well-known Olympians.
- Junior and disabled (hand-cycling) races on the same criterium circuit.
- A 13-km (8-mile) traffic-free loop for fun riders.

L'Etape du Tour

Annual charity-based event over one of the Tour de France stages for the year in question. It will take the riders several hours longer than the actual Tour riders to complete the stage, but the sense of achievement is still going to be huge.

There is a host of other one-day road races throughout the year for the more serious club cyclist, including magnificently named ones like the Dartmoor Demon, the Wye Valley Warrior, the South Downs Epic and the Peak District Punisher. End-of-season road races include the appropriately named Falling Leaves events, which is also the name of an autumnal mountain-bike and cyclo-cross endurance event against the backdrop of the New Forest. Or why not join the organised day trips over the Channel to try the French Resistance or the French Revolution? With some of these events, you can just turn up on the day and go. Others (like the French trips) will sell out their several hundred places within days. Check the www.ukcyclingevents.co.uk website for more information.

Longer events

John O'Groats to Land's End (JOGLE)
Also known as the 'End to End' or 'Deloitte Ride Across Britain', over 700 riders take part each year and more than 90 per cent of them make it to the finish line. If you're pushed for time, energy or willpower, you can confine yourself to the four-day Scottish or five-day English package. Or feel free to reverse the route and do the LEJOG as opposed to the JOGLE.

Bike Week
Bike Week sees a series of cycle-themed events take place around the UK for one week in the summer. Events include fun rides on streets closed to traffic, skills training, guided rides, commuter and workplace-based challenges, cycle fairs, themed rides, indoor track trials and even cycle speed dating. Check out www.bikeweek.org.uk for events near you.

Package holiday
Or if you want cycling to be an integral part of your well-earned holiday, search the web for the many tailored cycling tours that are available as a holiday package, at home or abroad.

BIKE RACING

When my legs hurt, I say 'Shut up, legs! Do what I tell you to do!'
JENS VOIGT, GERMAN PROFESSIONAL ROAD RACER
(AND CANDIDATE FOR MOST POPULAR GERMAN ON THE PLANET)

Road and track racing took off in a big way in continental Europe in the late nineteenth century, while Victorian Britain was still being positively Victorian. Without the backing of the establishment, bike racing didn't take off in Britain until much later. Speed was seen as a continental thing, best left to those volatile Europeans and their modern ways.

The world's first organised road race ran from Paris to Rouen in 1869, when the rules stated that riders were not allowed to use sails or be pulled by a dog. The race was won by an Englishman, James Moore, not least because he alone had the advantage of ball bearings in his moving parts (or, at least, in the moving parts of his bike). But even he had to get off and push his bike up the steeper climbs, gears not yet having been invented.

Some of the 'classic' one-day road races that are still going strong today followed soon after, including Liège-Bastogne-Liège (1894) and Paris-Roubaix (1896).

Stage racing over several days or even weeks took off with the inaugural Tour de France in 1903. Road races often finished with laps of a velodrome track, thereby combining the French love of both road and track racing.

The French and the Belgians were to dominate continental bike racing initially but they were soon joined by the Italians and later the Spaniards. A 'Foreign Legion' of English-speaking cyclists would gradually arrive on the European road scene in the later part of the twentieth century, not least the Americans and, most recently, the Brits, whose Olympic success has now spilt over into professional road racing.

The Olympics, as you might expect, has always been a rather more cosmopolitan affair than the European racing scene, with the early medal winners of the twentieth century including Greek, South African, Swedish, American and British riders.

But bike racing was to go really global in the twenty-first century. Starting in January 2008, the Tour Down Under in and around Adelaide has become the inaugural event of the UCI (Union Cycliste Internationale) calendar; the unprecedented road and track success of Great Britain at the 2008 Beijing and 2012 London Olympic Games looks like taking cycling to a whole new level; and BMX track racing became the newest sport of the Olympic Games in 2012, gripping millions around the world.

We will look at all of that, and more, in this chapter, but let us start where it all began – on the road.

Part 1: Road Racing

In this section we will look at some of the classic one-day road races as well as the longer stage races (also known as 'tours'). We will also cover road racing at the Olympic Games and World Championships.

The Classics

In a Nutshell
The classics are seriously tough one-day races that take place in western Europe in the spring and autumn, either side of the main stage-race season. If you're strong enough, and hard enough to sweat blood and risk broken bones, immortal glory awaits.

The five most prestigious classics are known as the 'Monuments', of which two are in Italy, two are in Belgium and one is in France:

Milan-San Remo
First raced in 1907, this is the first true classic of the season; it is known in Italian as *La Classica di Primavera* ('the spring classic'). It is also known as the 'sprinters' classic' because it often ends in a mass sprint. The great Belgian Eddy Merckx holds the record for most wins (seven). The German Erik Zabel would have won his fifth Milan-San Remo in 2004 had he not lifted his arms too early to celebrate his 'victory', thereby allowing himself to be pipped at the post.

Tour of Flanders

First run in 1913, the *Vlaanderens Mooiste* ('Flanders' finest') is one of the four 'cobbled classics', so called because of the stretches of cobbled roads that the riders have to contend with. The Tour of Flanders is said to be one of the most difficult races to ride, and therefore one of the best to win. A women's race has been run on the same day as the men's since 2004. Britain's Nicole Cooke won it in 2007 and the 2013 race was won by Marianne Vos, the Dutchwoman who is generally regarded to be the best bike rider of her generation.

Paris-Roubaix

First held in 1896, and nicknamed *L'enfer du Nord* ('Hell of the north'). Many riders will avoid it like the plague, because they don't want to risk early-season broken bones. For others, it is the ultimate prize. There are almost 30 bone-jarring cobbled sectors, including the Trouée d'Arenberg, a forested stretch of cobbles that dates back to the time of Napoleon I, and which is only opened twice a year – once to check that it is still far too dangerous to race on, the other for the race itself.

Liège-Bastogne-Liège

The third of the 'Ardennes classics', and the oldest classic of all, having been first run as a professional race in 1894. Known as *La Doyenne* ('Grand old dame'), this Belgian offering is arguably the toughest of the classics on account of its many hard climbs, particularly in the second half of the race. The route goes through the part of the Ardennes in which German and Allied forces fought out the Battle of the Bulge towards the end of World War Two. Most wins by a single rider is five, another record held by Eddy Merckx.

Giro di Lombardia

First took place in 1905, and known as *La Classica delle Foglie Morte* ('Classic of the Falling Leaves') because it is held in northern Italy in the autumn. Although the signature symbol of the race has become Lake Como, it is known as the 'climbers' classic' because of the use it makes of the nearby mountains, and it has in fact been won most times (five) by the great Italian climber of the 1940s and 1950s, Fausto Coppi.

The rider who has won the most Monuments by far (19) is Eddy Merckx. Only three riders, all Belgian, have won all five during the course of their careers: Roger de Vlaeminck, Rik van Looy and, of course, Eddy Merckx himself.

Re-cycled Fact

Il ne Passerieu pas

In 1907, the Frenchman Georges Passerieu still managed to win the Paris-Roubaix despite being stopped on his way in to the stadium by a gendarme who wanted to check he had the correct tax plate on his bike. Passerieu's language at the time was later reported to have been 'colourful'.

The Tours

Bicycle stage-racing doesn't come bigger than the three Grand Tours on the UCI (Union Cycliste Internationale) calendar:

- Tour de France
- Giro d'Italia
- Vuelta a España

> ### *In a Nutshell*
> *Only supreme athletes have the strength, stamina and sheer willpower to survive stage after stage, day after day, of fast racing, often combined with tough mountain climbing. Only the very best of those survivors have what it takes to win.*

They each last for three weeks: the Giro in May/June; the Tour in June/July; and the Vuelta in September. And they each have three main prizes: the general classification (GC) for the all-rounders; the points classification for the sprinters; and the 'King of the Mountains' classification for the specialist climbers. To give you an idea of the scale of these races, consider the following rough statistics over the three-week period:

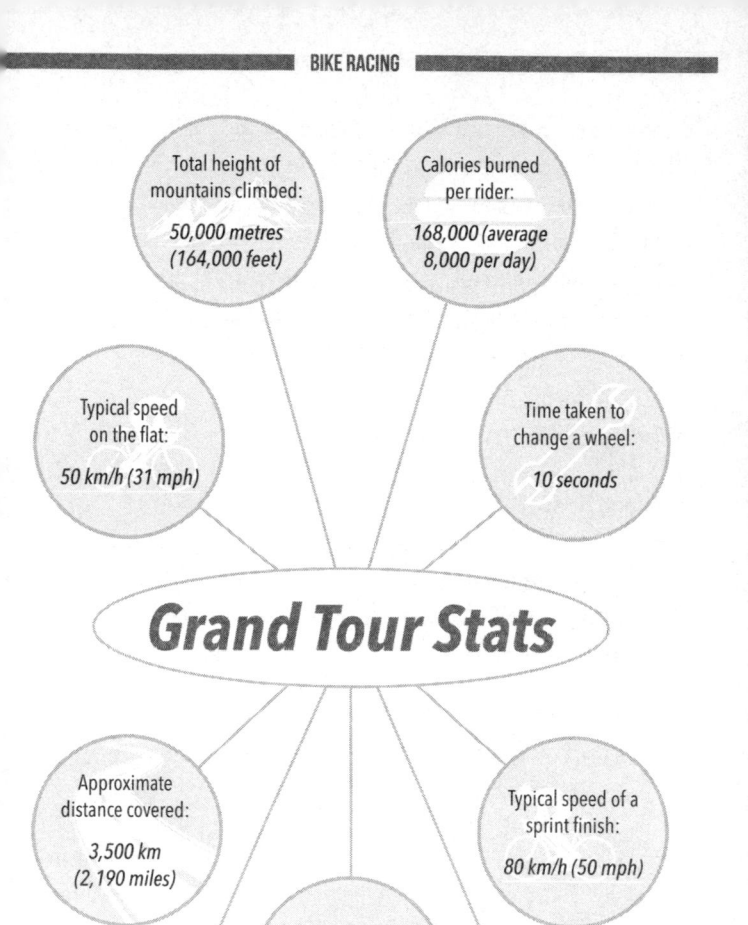

Total height of mountains climbed:

50,000 metres (164,000 feet)

Calories burned per rider:

168,000 (average 8,000 per day)

Typical speed on the flat:

50 km/h (31 mph)

Time taken to change a wheel:

10 seconds

Grand Tour Stats

Approximate distance covered:

3,500 km (2,190 miles)

Typical speed of a sprint finish:

80 km/h (50 mph)

Typical speed on mountain descents:

100km/h (62 mph)

Energy drinks consumed per rider:

300

Bike wheels used per rider:

20

Other 'elite' (but much shorter) stage races include the Tour Down Under, Paris-Nice and the Critérium du Dauphiné. The next tour category (classified as 'majors') includes races as far apart as the Tour of California, the Tour of Langkawi (Malaysia) and the Tour of Turkey, and the bottom tour category includes the Tour of Britain.

The most important stage race on the women's circuit is currently the Giro Rosa in Italy (previously known as the Giro d'Italia Femminile).

The Grand Tours

Tour de France
First run in 1903 and still the biggest and best bike race in the world, the Tour de France remains to cycling what the World Cup is to football, what Wimbledon is to tennis and what the Super Bowl is to American football.

> *The Tour de France produces in me such persistent satisfaction*
> *that my saliva flows in imperceptible but stubborn streams.*
> SALVADOR DALÍ, CATALAN SURREALIST PAINTER

Yellow jersey
The symbolic prize of the general classification (GC) is the coveted *maillot jaune* (yellow jersey), yellow being the colour of the pages of the *L'Auto* newspaper owned by the Tour's founder Henri Desgrange. Today the race always finishes on the Champs-Elysées in Paris after around 3,500 km (2,190 miles) of time trials, flat stages and mountain climbs.

Four riders have won the yellow jersey competition five times:

- Jacques Anquetil (France)
- Bernard Hinault (France)
- Eddy Merckx (Belgium)
- Miguel Indurain (Spain)

Bradley Wiggins became the first British winner in 2012, the latest in a long line of specialist time triallists who have managed to hang on in the mountains to the advantages they gained against the clock back at sea level.

Brian Robinson was the first Briton to finish a Tour de France, in 1955, and the first to win a stage, in 1958.

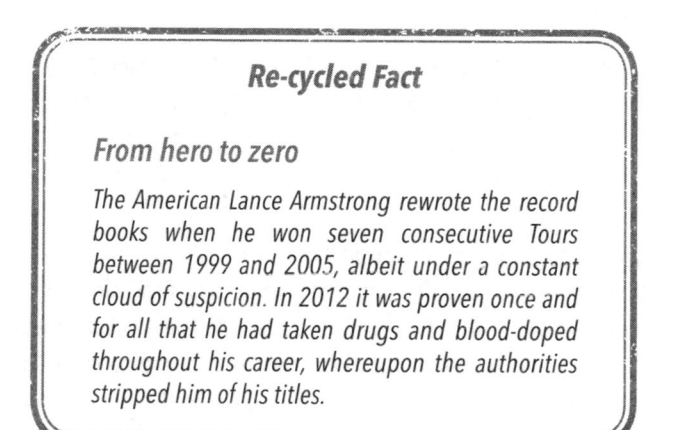

Re-cycled Fact

From hero to zero

The American Lance Armstrong rewrote the record books when he won seven consecutive Tours between 1999 and 2005, albeit under a constant cloud of suspicion. In 2012 it was proven once and for all that he had taken drugs and blood-doped throughout his career, whereupon the authorities stripped him of his titles.

Green jersey (points classification)

British rider Mark Cavendish, aka the 'Manx Missile', is smashing the Tour sprint records as he chalks up stage win after stage win with his lightning bursts of speed to the finish line. The German Erik Zabel remains the rider who has won the most green jersey competitions, with a record six (consecutive) wins between 1996 and 2001.

Polka-dot jersey
(King of the Mountains classification)

Legendary Tour climbers include Lucien van Impe (Belgium), Federico Bahamontes (Spain) and Fausto Coppi (Italy). The Frenchman Richard Virenque won more King of the Mountains titles than anyone else (seven), but his reputation was tarnished as a central figure in the infamous Festina doping affair in 1998. Scottish rider Robert Millar won the King of the Mountains title in 1984 and remains the only rider from an English-speaking country to do so.

Re-cycled Fact

Vive la Grande Bretagne!

In 2007, when the Tour de France visited Britain for the third time, millions lined the streets of London and the roads to Canterbury, an indication that road racing had finally entered the British consciousness at something like the levels enjoyed in mainland Europe over the previous hundred years and more.

Giro d'Italia

First run in 1908 to boost sales of *La Gazzetta dello Sport* newspaper, the Giro follows the same general format as the Tour de France. The traditional finish is in Milan, where the GC winner is awarded the *maglia rosa* (pink jersey), pink being the colour of the pages of *La Gazzetta*.

Three riders have won the Giro five times:

- Alfredo Binda (Italy)
- Fausto Coppi (Italy)
- Eddy Merckx (Belgium)

Binda was the first Italian cycling superstar and he dominated the Giro in the 1920s. Gino Bartali, who was Coppi's great rival in the 1940s, holds the record for most King of the Mountains titles in the Giro (seven), with Robert Millar providing a solitary British win in 1987.

No tourists were harmed in the running of this race

One of the most thrilling stages ever in the Giro was a time trial in 1978 that ran alongside the canals of Venice before finishing in the tourist trap of Piazza San Marco (St Mark's Square). It was won by legendary Italian sprinter and classics rider Francesco Moser.

Re-cycled Fact

In nomine Patri...

It is traditional for the Pope to bless the maglia rosa ahead of the Giro each year, and he will often also receive the riders at the start. Pope Pius XII made an exception in 1954 due to Fausto Coppi's very public marital indiscretions (adultery was still a criminal as well as a moral offence in Italy at the time). As a result, many of the Italian tifosi (fans) turned their backs on, or even spat at, Coppi during the ensuing race.

Vuelta a España

Established in 1935 to boost sales of the *Informaciones* newspaper, the Vuelta also follows the format of the Tour de France. Jersey colours have changed over the years but the GC winner is currently awarded the *jersey rojo* (red jersey) following the race's traditional finish in Madrid. Two riders have won the Vuelta three times: Tony Rominger of Switzerland, with three consecutive wins between 1992 and 1994, and Roberto Heras of Spain between 2000 and 2004. Ireland's Sean Kelly won it in 1988 and remains the only rider from an English-speaking country to have won the Vuelta.

Kelly and France's Laurent Jalabert have been the Vuelta's top sprinters, having won four points classifications apiece.

The Spaniard José Luis Laguía has been the Vuelta's top climber, with a record five King of the Mountains titles.

Re-cycled Fact

Grand Tour trebles

Only a paltry 32 riders have completed the Tour de France, the Giro d'Italia and the Vuelta a España in the same year. Most GC victories across all three is a record held, unsurprisingly, by Eddy Merckx (eleven). Next in line are Frenchmen Bernard Hinault (ten) and Jacques Anquetil (eight).

The other Tours

Tour Down Under

First run in 1999, it has already been promoted to the highest-ranking professional race outside Europe. Aside from the Tour de France, it also attracts the biggest crowds anywhere in the world – almost 800,000 over the six days of the event in and around Adelaide.

In order to save transportation costs for the international teams, this Tour has no time trials (which, of course, require different bikes and clothing), and as there are no hills worth speaking about in this part of South Australia, most stages will finish in a mass sprint. The biggest issue for the riders is the searing January heat. Three riders have won the race twice: Aussies Stuart O'Grady and Simon Gerrans, and German André Greipel.

Re-cycled Fact

Hero for a week

A wonderful tradition of the Tour Down Under is that the fans choose an unknown, non-English-speaking, domestique *(a rider who supports the more important team members by, for example, carrying their water during the race) and treat him as if he were a star. They mob him in hotels and paint his name on the roads on each day of the race.*

Paris-Nice

First held in 1933, the week-long 'Race to the Sun' in March has normally finished with a mass sprint on the Promenade des Anglais, or on the nearby hill-climb of the Col d'Eze. The Irishman Sean Kelly has won the race the most times, with an astonishing seven consecutive wins between 1982 and 1988, during which entire period he was also ranked number one rider in the world.

Briton Tom Simpson won the race in 1967, not long before the Tour de France that year would claim his life on Mont Ventoux in the French Alps. He remained the only Briton to have won the Paris-Nice classic until Bradley Wiggins achieved the feat in 2012.

Critérium du Dauphiné

Run since 1947 in the first half of June over eight stages in the mountainous Dauphiné region of France, this is the last important race before the Tour de France each year. As such, it is used by many of the top riders to put the finishing touches to their Tour de France preparations. Four riders have won the classic three times: Nello Lauredi, Charly Mottet, Bernard Hinault (all France) and Luis Ocaña (Spain). Three Brits have won the race: Brian Robinson in 1961, Robert Millar in 1990 and Bradley Wiggins in 2011. Wiggins won it again in 2012 before going on to win the Tour de France itself.

Got Milk?

Following previous incarnations that included the Milk Race and the Kellogg's Tour, the Tour of Britain is now an eight-day stage event held in September. In 2012, Jonathan Tiernan-Locke became the first Briton to win the Tour of Britain in its current form and the first Briton to win any British tour since Chris Lillywhite won the Milk Race in 1993.

Mark Cavendish won the sprinters' points classification in 2007, while riding for T-Mobile. While riding for Team Sky, and as reigning World Road Race Champion, he took three stage wins in 2012, including the final sprint on the final day up Guildford's cobbled High Street.

The 2013 route takes in the Scottish Borders, the Lake District, Snowdonia National Park and a summit finish on Dartmoor, before finishing with a flourish on London's Whitehall.

Giro Rosa

Formerly known as the Giro d'Italia Femminile, as of 2013 the race was rebranded as the Giro Rosa ('pink tour') and reduced to eight days. Nicknamed the *Giro Donne* ('women's tour'), it is the only Grand Tour left in the women's calendar after lack of sponsorship saw the Tour de France Féminin and the Tour de L'Aude fall by the wayside in recent years.

First raced in 1988, the Giro Donne has been won most times (five) by Italian rider Fabiana Luperini. Nicole Cooke is the only British rider to have won, in 2004, and Britain's Emma Pooley finished runner-up in 2011 and 2012, on both occasions to the top women's rider of recent years, the Dutchwoman Marianne Vos.

Olympics (road)

In a Nutshell

Different forms of individual and team road races came and went over the first hundred years of the modern Olympics, but since 1996 only individual road races and time trials have been held.

World domination

Great Britain has at times punched way above its weight and only France has won more cycling medals in the entire history of the modern Olympics. GB won a record 36 cycling medals at the London 1908 games and again secured world domination a hundred years later in Beijing, with 25 medals, which it followed with another 24 at London in 2012.

Event:	Road race (men)
Introduced:	Athens, Greece (1896)
First winner:	Aristidis Konstantinidis (Greece)
Most wins:	No multiple winners
Other notable winners:	Fabio Casartelli (Italy)
Fascinating facts:	The road cycling event in Athens in 1896 was an 87-km (54-mile) race to Marathon and back.

Three years after winning his gold medal in Barcelona in 1992, Italian Fabio Casartelli lost his life after hitting his head on a concrete barrier on a mountain descent of the Tour de France.

Bradley Wiggins, Chris Froome et al were meant to deliver red-hot favourite Mark Cavendish to the front in time for him to sprint to glory in the 2012 race in London, but they lost out after getting caught in the pack.

Event:	Road race (women)
Introduced:	Los Angeles, California, USA (1984)
First winner:	Connie Carpenter (USA)
Most wins:	No multiple winners
Other notable winners:	Jeannie Longo (France)
	Nicole Cooke (GB)
	Marianne Vos (Netherlands)
Fascinating facts:	Nicole Cooke's gold medal in Beijing in 2008 was GB's 200th in the modern Olympics.

THE JOY OF CYCLING

Event:	Time trial (men)
Introduced:	Atlanta, Georgia, USA (1996)
First winner:	Miguel Indurain (Spain)
Most wins (2):	Viatcheslav Ekimov (Russia)
Other notable winners:	Fabian Cancellara (Switzerland) Bradley Wiggins (GB)
Fascinating facts:	The Russian Viatcheslav Ekimov won gold at Sydney in 2000 and at Athens in 2004, but he didn't receive his Athens gold until 2012, after the American Tyler Hamilton, who had been first over the line, finally confessed to doping throughout his career.

Event:	Time trial (women)
Introduced:	Atlanta, Georgia, USA (1996)
First winner:	Zulfiya Zabirova (Russia)
Most wins (2):	Leontien van Moorsel (Netherlands) Kristin Armstrong (USA)
Fascinating facts:	Dutch rider Leontien van Moorsel pulled out of professional cycling in 1994, suffering from anorexia, but recovered to resume one of the most successful cycling careers in history, including racking up a total of six Olympic medals.

World Championships (road)

In a Nutshell

The World Championships are held annually at different venues around the world. The highlights of the week-long programme are the men's and women's single-stage road races and time trials.

Event:	Road race (men)
Introduced:	Nurbürgring, Germany (1927)
First winner:	Alfredo Binda (Italy)
Most wins (3):	Alfredo Binda (Italy) Óscar Freire (Spain) Eddy Merckx (Belgium) Rik van Steenbergen (Belgium)
Other notable winners:	Fausto Coppi (Italy) Tom Simpson (GB) Bernard Hinault (France) Greg LeMond (USA) Stephen Roche (Ireland) Lance Armstrong (USA) Cadel Evans (Australia) Mark Cavendish (GB)
Fascinating facts:	Tom Simpson won the race for Britain in San Sebastián in northern Spain in 1965, and remained the only British winner until Mark Cavendish finally repeated the feat in Copenhagen in 2011. Between them, Belgians and Italians have won well over half the gold medals on offer.

Event:	Road race (women)
Introduced:	Reims, France (1958)
First winner:	Elsy Jacobs (Luxembourg)
Most wins (5):	Jeannie Longo (France)
Other notable winners:	Nicole Cooke (GB)
	Marianne Vos (Netherlands)
Fascinating facts:	Mandy Jones won for Great Britain at the age of 20 on home soil at Goodwood, West Sussex, in 1982. It was the only major win of her career.
	In 2008 Nicole Cooke became the only rider (male or female) to be World Road Race Champion and Olympic Road Race Champion in the same year.
	Dutch superstar Marianne Vos won gold in 2006 and 2012, and silver in each of the five years in between.

Event:	Time trial (men)
Introduced:	Catania, Italy (1994)
First winner:	Chris Boardman (GB)
Most wins (4):	Fabian Cancellara (Switzerland)
Other notable winners:	Miguel Indurain (Spain)
Fascinating facts:	Fabian Cancellara won his four gold medals in the space of five years between 2006 and 2010.

Event:	Time trial (women)
Introduced:	Agrigento, Italy (1994)
First winner:	Karen Kurreck (USA)
Most wins (4):	Jeannie Longo (France)
Other notable winners:	Emma Pooley (GB)
Fascinating facts:	Emma Pooley won Britain's only gold medal to date in Melbourne in 2010.

Re-cycled Fact

Over the rainbow

In common with other cycling disciplines, the Road Race and Time Trial World Champions wear the coveted 'rainbow jersey' for the whole of the year in which they reign. In fact, the jersey is predominantly white and contains only five colours in horizontal stripes – the same five colours as appear on the Olympic flag.

Cycling at the Paralympic Games

In a Nutshell

Cycling became a Paralympic sport at the New York/ Stoke Mandeville Games in 1984, and a handcycling programme was added at Athens in 2000. Road and track events now largely mirror those of the Olympics for all three disability groups (vision impaired, cerebral palsy and wheelchair), except that visually impaired sprinters ride on tandems so that they can have sighted guides.

Great Britain overtook Australia as the dominant force in Paralympics cycling at Beijing in 2008, and again topped the medal table at London in 2012. British multiple medal winners include David Stone, Darren Kenny, Jody Cundy and Sarah Storey (see the Hall of Fame at the end of this chapter for more information on Sarah Storey).

Re-cycled Fact

The Comeback King

The London 2012 Paralympic Games witnessed the astonishing feat of the Italian former racing driver, Alex Zanardi, as he handbiked to two gold medals 11 years after losing both his legs following a horrific crash in an IndyCar race.

Part 2: Track

In this section we will look at the unusual world of track cycling, again covering the Olympic Games and the World Championships.

Olympics (Track)

In a Nutshell
Different Olympic track events have come and gone since 1896, but they were finally standardised in 2012 for men and women as the keirin, omnium, team pursuit, individual sprint and team sprint.

Clean sweep

Team GB won an impressive seven out of ten track cycling golds at Beijing in 2008 *and* London in 2012, but that was nothing compared to the statistics of the USA team in 1904. Only 18 track cyclists entered the games held in St Louis and they were all American. Over the course of the seven events held, the USA, rather unsurprisingly, took seven gold, seven silver and seven bronze. This is a record not likely to be beaten!

EVENT	GOLD	SILVER	BRONZE
1/4 mile	USA	USA	USA
1/3 mile	USA	USA	USA
1/2 mile	USA	USA	USA
1 mile	USA	USA	USA
2 miles	USA	USA	USA
5 miles	USA	USA	USA
25 miles	USA	USA	USA

As it is easy to become confused about what is going on in the constantly changing world of track cycling, here is a summary of the different track cycling disciplines as currently constituted:

Keirin

Japanese for 'racing wheels', the keirin started in Japan as a betting sport in 1948 and only became an Olympic event (for men) at Sydney in 2000. Riders stay in predetermined order behind a motorised pacer (known as a 'derny') until sprinting for victory over the last 600-700 metres (375-440 yards) at speeds of up to 70 kph (43 mph). In 2012 Victoria Pendleton (GB) won the first-ever keirin for women in the Olympics and Chris Hoy (GB) successfully defended the title he had won in Beijing four years earlier.

Omnium

Consists of six sub-events:

- Flying lap (individually, against the clock).
- Points race: a mass-start multiple-lap race of 30 km (18.75 miles) for men and 20 km (12.5 miles) for women – points are awarded for intermediate sprints and for lapping other riders.
- Elimination race: sometimes referred to as 'devil take the hindmost', as the rider to cross the line at the end of each lap (or a predetermined number of laps) is eliminated until the few remaining riders sprint to the finish.
- Individual pursuit: where two riders start on opposite sides of the track and race until they reach their respective finishing lines at the end of the race distance, or until one catches the other (hence 'pursuit'). Was previously an event in its own right before being subsumed into the omnium in 2012.
- Scratch race: another mass-start multiple-lap race, but results are determined on a simple first-past-the-post basis – 15 km (9.3 miles) for men and 10 km (8 miles) for women.

- Time trial: racing individually against the clock from a standing start over 1 km for men and 500 m for women.

The Danish rider Lasse Norman Hansen won the inaugural men's event in 2012 and Laura Trott took gold for Britain in the inaugural women's competition.

Team pursuit

This is similar to the individual pursuit in the omnium, but with teams of four (men) or three (women) starting from opposite sides of the track. Teams ride in a line to minimise drag and take turns pacemaking at the front. Finishing time is when the front wheel of the third rider crosses the line, so it is not uncommon in the men's race for the fourth rider to take a 'death pull' at the front and then peel off exhausted while the remaining three sprint together for the line.

Introduced to the Olympics in 1908 for men only, Italy has won the most gold medals (seven), followed by Germany (five). Great Britain won the men's event in 2008 and 2012, and the inaugural women's event in 2012.

Individual sprint

This is a one-against-one sprint, except the sprinting doesn't start until one of the riders breaks for the line at the end of the cat-and-mouse tactical game that precedes it on the banks of the velodrome. Frenchmen have won more gold medals (seven) than anyone else since 1896, and Chris Hoy (Beijing, 2008) and Jason Kenny (London, 2012) have both won for Britain in recent times. Introduced for women at Seoul in 1988, the event has enjoyed epic battles in recent Olympics between British rider Victoria Pendleton and her arch-rival, the Australian Anna Meares (Pendleton took gold in Beijing and Meares reversed the positions four years later in London).

Re-cycled Fact

Time out!

Nobody won the 1,000-metre sprint gold medal in 1908 after it was declared null and void because the four finalists (three British and one French) exceeded the time limit of 1 minute 45 seconds for the race. They had got so caught up in the cat-and-mouse tactical battle that they forgot to dash for the line.

The seemingly curious behaviour of the riders in the early stages of these races, as they vary speed between slow, 'nudging forward' and stationary (they balance the bike in a stationary position by converting the tension of their single-speed drive train into side-to-side motion), is designed to keep the opponent either in front (in order to benefit from an aerodynamic slipstream in the sprint) or higher up the velodrome bank (in order to force the opponent into a wider racing line).

Team sprint

The name is misleading, because this is a three-man or two-woman team time trial. In the case of the men's race, the first-lap pacemaker peels away at the end of that lap, the second-lap pacemaker does likewise at the end of the second lap, and the third man sprints the final lap on his own. Two teams race simultaneously, starting at opposite sides of the track as in a pursuit race.

Introduced as a men's event in 2000, Team GB took gold in Beijing and London, whereas Germany won the inaugural women's event in 2012.

Re-cycled Fact

The 'Pringle'

The award-winning London 2012 velodrome was the first Olympic Park venue to be completed. Aerodynamic and energy-efficient, it was a triumph of engineering known affectionately as the 'Pringle' on account of its shape. Fifty-six kilometres (35 miles) of Siberian Pine and 350,000 nails were used in the construction of the 250-metre track.

World Championships (Track)

In a Nutshell

Held annually around the world, the format is very similar to that of the Olympics, except the scratch and points events remain as individual competitions as well as being components of the omnium, and the men's Madison event (contested by up to 18 teams of two riders who take turns to race the intermediate sprints in which the points are won and lost) is alive and well.

The men's championships were inaugurated in Chicago in 1893, and the first women's events took place in Paris in 1958. France dominated the championships for a great many years, not least because they had a 14-times men's champion in Arnaud Tournant, and a 13-times women's champion in Jeannie Longo. In more recent years, with so many great cycling stars at its disposal, Great Britain has taken over as the dominant team and has enjoyed more rivalry with Australia than with France.

> ### *Re-cycled Fact*
>
> #### *Like waiting for a bus*
>
> *In the 2013 World Championships in Minsk, Belarus, Martyn Irvine ended Ireland's 116-year wait for a medal, winning a silver in the individual pursuit. Ireland had to wait less than 116 years for its second medal, as Irvine returned an hour later to take gold in the scratch event (first past the post after 60 laps, or 15 km/9.3 miles).*

Part 3: BMX

In a Nutshell

BMX is short for bicycle motocross and BMX track is a craze that swept 1970s America before becoming a World Championship event in 1982 and a full-blown Olympic event at Beijing in 2008. Riders bolt from a raised starting gate to race against one another for about 40 seconds on a rollercoaster of a course that includes wave-like bumps and berms (banked corners).

The USA leads the BMX Track World Championship medal table with 24 golds, ahead of France (21). The magnificently named American, Randy Stumpfhauser, tops the men's individual medal table, and the most successful women's rider is Gabriela Díaz of Argentina.

British rider Shanaze Reade has won the women's BMX Track World Championship title three times (2007, 2008, 2010), whilst also finding time to partner Victoria Pendleton to World Championship gold (twice) and silver in the women's team sprint in the velodrome, a very different discipline to BMX track racing.

Māris Štrombergs of Latvia became the first men's Olympic BMX champion in Beijing, and Anne-Caroline Chausson of France became the first women's champion. Because the women's final was held first, Chausson got the honour of winning the first gold medal of the Olympics' newest sport. Shanaze Reade, the reigning world champion at the time, fell in the final after clipping Chausson's rear wheel at the last turn.

BMX mongrel

BMX bikes were originally Schwinn Sting-Rays that were modified by swapping out the seat, handlebars, grips, forks, wheels, brakes and tyres, and then removing the fenders, kickstand, chain guard and reflectors. In other words, there wasn't much left of the Sting-Ray by the time it became a BMX, and even then it remained a bit heavy and clunky for the purpose of replicating motocross racing. Gary Turner (of GT Bicycles fame) was an aircraft and drag-racing welder who saw the inherent nonsense of this and designed the first production BMX in 1973.

Part 4: Mountain Bike

In a Nutshell

Nerves of steel and bags of stamina are required to negotiate cross-country courses that entail rocky paths, tricky climbs and technical descents over an elapsed time of up to two hours. There are stations at designated points on the course for riders to make repairs to their bikes and take on much-needed sustenance. Other disciplines include downhill (an individual time trial), four-cross (downhill racing with four riders at a time), trial riding (passing through obstacle courses without a foot touching the ground) and cross-country marathon.

Like BMX track, mountain-bike racing is a young sport that kicked off in 1970s America. The first World Championships were held in 1990 in Durango, Colorado, USA, and have been held once in the UK, at Fort William in Scotland, in 2007. The sport entered the Olympics at Atlanta in 1996.

Julien Absalon of France has won most men's cross-country world titles (four), and Gunn-Rita Dahle Flesjå of Norway tops the women's list (also with four gold medals). Cadel Evans, the first Australian winner of the Tour de France in 2010, won the Mountain Bike World Cup (which is a series event, different from the World Championship) in 1998 and 1999, and rode for Australia in the mountain bike event at the Sydney 2000 Olympics.

The godfather of mountain biking

We have already seen how Gary Fisher's name became synonymous with the mountain bike, as he is considered to be one of its inventors. He himself started competing in road and track races in 1963 at the age of 12, but was suspended from racing as a 17-year-old for having long hair and it was four years before the moronic rule was repealed. He went on to win races that included the brutal TransAlp, the original epic mountain bike race in Europe (still run annually), and in 1977 he set the record of 4 minutes 22 seconds on the infamous Repack Downhill (a tortuous descent of 400 metres – 1,300 feet – in just over 1.2 km – 2 miles) in Fairfax, California.

Frenchman Nicolas Vouilloz reigns supreme in the World Championship downhill list, with seven world titles in eight years between 1995 and 2002. Vouilloz's compatriot, Anne-Caroline Chausson, has done even better, winning nine titles in ten years between 1996 and 2005. As we have already seen, she also went on to win the first-ever BMX track gold medal at the Beijing Olympics in 2008. Britain has produced three men's downhill world champions: Gee Atherton (2008), Steve Peat (2009) and Danny Hart (2011); and two women's downhill champions: Rachel Atherton (2008) and Tracy Moseley (2010).

At the Olympics, Julien Absalon has won two men's gold medals (Athens 2004 and Beijing 2008) and Italian rider Paola Pezzo has won two women's titles (Atlanta 1996 and Sydney 2000). The London 2012 cross-country venue was at Hadleigh Farm in Essex, on land owned by the Salvation Army. Julie Bresset of France won the women's race, and Jaroslav Kulhavý of the Czech Republic won the men's after a thrilling sprint finish.

Part 5: Cyclo-cross

In a Nutshell
A winter sport that consists of laps of a cross-country track, with races lasting for about an hour. Cyclo-cross differs from mountain-bike racing in that riders have to cross obstacles that require dismounting and the carrying of bikes over their shoulders (normally for about 5 per cent of the race). Aerobic endurance and bike-handling skills are of the essence.

Cyclo-cross is thought to have originated in France and Belgium in the early 1900s as riders raced each other to the next town over roads, through fields, across streams and over hedges or fences. These men were referred to as *coureurs de steeple* ('steeplechasers') because a church steeple was often all they had to aim for.

The sport grew slowly but surely until the first World Championships were held in Paris in 1950. It then took off in America at the same time as BMX and mountain biking did in the 1970s, but the championships never left mainland Europe until 2013 when they finally made it across the Atlantic to Louisville, Kentucky.

The Belgian Erik de Vlaeminck has won most gold medals in the men's competition, with seven titles between 1966 and 1973. The women's World Championships were inaugurated in 2000 and were won six times in eight years, between 2006 and 2013, by Dutch super-rider Marianne Vos.

One of the longest and hardest cyclo-cross races in the world is the Three Peaks Cyclo-cross, which has been run in Yorkshire since 1961. Local runner Rob Jebb has dominated the men's race in the twenty-first century, and Louise Robinson (daughter of Brian Robinson, the first Briton to win a stage of the Tour de France in 1958) has won the women's race a record five times.

Merry Veldrijden

Literally 'field-riding', veldrijden is Flemish for cyclo-cross and the Belgians of the Flanders region in particular go mad for it. And I don't just mean the riders who compete at everything from junior to elite level, I mean also the hordes of spectators who turn out in all conditions to watch the 'weekend warriors' battle through mud, snow and ice. Even Christmas Day is an important fixture in the world of veldrijden.

Part 6: Cycle Speedway

In a Nutshell
As with the motorcycle version, four riders race individual and team events over four laps around an oval track. Physical contact is legal and often necessary to stay on the bike or get the better of an opponent.

Similar in format to motorcycle speedway, the cycle version is said to have taken off in post-war Britain as a way for youngsters with not much else to do to enjoy themselves. They cleared tracks through the rubble of bomb sites and used bikes that were not otherwise roadworthy. Within five years there were 200 clubs in east London alone and the sport had spread around the country.

After it had found its way to the Netherlands, an international between that country and England in 1950 at Earls Court attracted 10,000 spectators. But, as bomb sites were cleared for fresh building and young men were drafted for national service, the sport fell away, but never entirely.

Resurrected in the 1970s, the sport has since grown internationally and now includes Russia, the USA and Australia. Men's World Championships have been held every two years since 1958 and Great Britain has produced nine champions, including three-times winner Dave Hemsley, and Jim Varnish, father of Olympic track sprinter Jess Varnish. Laura Watson took the inaugural women's World Championship for Britain in 2013, two seconds ahead of fellow Sheffield cyclist Vicky Brown.

Many cycle speedway riders go on to other disciplines, most notably Australian Brett Aitken, who went on to win gold, silver and bronze Olympic track-cycling medals for his country.

Part 7: Hall of Fame

The list of multiple-race-winning cyclists is a long one, so the following 'Hall of Fame' celebrates the achievements of just a few of those who have succeeded more than once, more often than not over a long number of years, and very often across more than one cycling discipline:

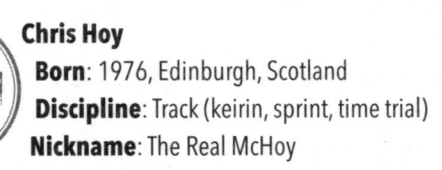

Chris Hoy
Born: 1976, Edinburgh, Scotland
Discipline: Track (keirin, sprint, time trial)
Nickname: The Real McHoy

Chris Hoy is the most successful Olympic cyclist in history, and the most successful British Olympian of all time, with six gold medals and one silver. In the track events he specialised in (sprint, time trial and keirin), the Edinburgh-born rider also amassed 11 World Championship titles. As BBC Sports Personality of the Year 2008, he was only the second cyclist ever to win the award (43 years after Tom Simpson had won it in 1965). Knighted in the 2009 New Year Honours List and immortalised in the Sir Chris Hoy Velodrome built for the 2014 Commonwealth Games in Glasgow.

Bradley Wiggins
Born: 1980, Ghent, Belgium
Disciplines: Track (Madison, pursuit) and road
Nickname: Wiggo

A rare breed of cyclist who has enjoyed success on the track and on the road, Wiggins is a cycling legend who took to the sport after watching Chris Boardman win gold at the 1992 Barcelona Olympics. He has won three Olympic track gold medals, plus six World Championship track titles. His specialist track events were individual and team pursuit, and the Madison.

Having made the difficult switch to road racing, Wiggins swept all before him in 2012, winning the Paris-Nice, the Tour de Romandie, the Critérium du Dauphiné, the Tour de France (as the first-ever British winner of the race) and the Olympic time trial. This unprecedented level of success brought him the BBC Sports Personality of the Year award for 2012 and a knighthood in the 2013 New Year Honours List.

Mark Cavendish
Born: 1985, Douglas, Isle of Man
Disciplines: Road and track (Madison, points, scratch)
Nickname: The Manx Missile

Completing the trio of Britain's twenty-first-century cycling superheroes, the 'Manx Missile' is the fastest road sprinter ever, having earlier cut his teeth on the track with two world titles in the Madison in 2005 and 2008.

The explosive bursts of speed that propel him to the finishing line have already resulted in over 20 Tour de France stage wins – at the time of writing only Eddy Merckx, Bernard Hinault and André Leducq have won more than him, but nobody has won more in terms of mass-finish sprints alone. In 2008, he took two stages in the Giro and four in the Tour at the age of just 23. He blasted his way to six more Tour stage wins in 2009 alone. In 2011 he became the first-ever British winner of the Tour de France green jersey, and in the same year ended Britain's 46-year wait for a road race world champion. He won the BBC Sports Personality of the Year trophy in 2011, with an astonishing 49 per cent of the public vote, and was also awarded an MBE. In 2012 he became the first rider to win the final stage of the Tour de France on the Champs-Elysées in four consecutive years.

Eddy Merckx
Born: 1945, Meensel, Belgium
Discipline: Road
Nickname: The Cannibal

Widely regarded to be the greatest rider of all time, Merckx lived up to his nickname of 'the Cannibal' in the 1960s and 1970s by gobbling up kilometres, trophies and records in a way that is unlikely ever to be surpassed. During his astonishing career he won the Tour de France and the Giro d'Italia five times each, three World Championships and one Vuelta a España. He is one of only two riders (along with Stephen Roche of Ireland) to win cycling's Triple Crown by winning the Tour, the Giro and the World Championship in the same year (1974). He also won all five of the Monument classics at least twice each.

In 1996 the King of Belgium awarded him the ceremonial title of 'Baron', and in 2000 he was chosen as Belgium's Sports Figure of the Century.

Marianne Vos
Born: 1987, 's-Hertogenbosch, the Netherlands
Discipline: Road, track (points, scratch, Madison),
cyclo-cross, mountain biking
Nickname: *Vosje* ('Little Fox')

An unstoppable force in women's racing, the Dutch superwoman has won world titles in three different cycling disciplines: road, track and cyclo-cross. Having already been Dutch junior mountain bike champion (four times) and Dutch junior road race champion (twice), she became road-race world champion and cyclo-cross world champion in 2006, aged just 19, and added her first track World Championship two years later. She then added Olympic track gold in Beijing in 2008.

In 2012 she surpassed even her own ridiculously high standards, winning the Olympic road race, the World Championship road race, the Giro d'Italia Femminile and three World Cup races in a single year. As the dominant force in women's road racing, she ended that year as world number one in the UCI rankings by a long way.

Fabian Cancellara
Born: 1981, Wohlen bei Bern, Switzerland
Discipline: Road
Nickname: Spartacus

Nicknamed Spartacus on account of his fighting spirit, the Swiss rider has achieved phenomenal success as a time triallist and as a classics specialist. As a time triallist, he is a four-times world champion. He has won the opening stage of the Tour de France five times, and has led the race for 28 days in total, which is a record for any rider who hasn't won the Tour. He also won Olympic time-trial gold in 2008 in Beijing. As far as the classics are concerned (at the time of writing) he has won Paris-Roubaix three times, the Tour of Flanders twice and the Milan-San Remo once.

Jeannie Longo
Born: 1958, Annecy, France
Discipline: Road, track, mountain biking
Nickname: The Cannibal

The appropriately named French rider competed in a staggering seven Olympic Games, winning four medals, including one gold. At her final Olympics in Beijing in 2008, she missed out on a fifth medal by two seconds, notwithstanding that many of her fellow competitors had not been born when she raced in her first Olympics in Los Angeles in 1984. She was world road race champion five times, road time trial world champion four times and a track world champion on four occasions. She achieved the women's world hour record in 2000 in Mexico City, and proved her versatility yet further by winning silver in 1993 in the Mountain Bike & Trials World Championships.

Longo has often been acclaimed as the female equivalent of the great Eddy Merckx, hence the shared nickname.

Sean Kelly
Born: 1956, Carrick-on-Suir, Ireland
Discipline: Road
Nickname: King Kelly

Irish rider Sean Kelly didn't just win four green jersey competitions at the Tour de France; he was one of the most successful riders of the 1980s and one of the great classics winners of all time, including Paris-Nice a staggering seven years in a row. He was the first rider to be ranked number one when world rankings were introduced to cycling in 1984, a position he held on to for a record-breaking six years.

Sarah Storey
Born: 1977, Manchester
Discipline: Road and track (pursuit)
Nickname: (None)

A remarkable British Paralympian who won five gold, eight silver and three bronze swimming medals before switching to cycling for the Beijing Olympics in 2008. Storey won two cycling golds in Beijing, and followed them up with another four cycling gold medals at London 2012, making a staggering total of 22 Paralympic medals to date. She has won national track titles against non-disabled cyclists and has similarly represented England at the Commonwealth Games. She was awarded the MBE in 1998 and the OBE in 2009, before being made a Dame in the 2013 New Year Honours List.

Chris Boardman
Born: 1968, Hoylake, England
Discipline: Road and track (pursuit)
Nicknames: The Professor; Mr Prologue

The engaging British rider, now a popular TV presenter, won the individual-pursuit track gold medal at the Barcelona Olympics in 1992, and went on to become a three-times world champion in track pursuit (twice) and road time trial.

He won a total of three Tour de France prologue time trials (Lille in 1994, Rouen in 1997 and Dublin in 1998) and, because prologues always take place on day one of the Tour, these wins guaranteed that he got to wear the coveted *maillot jaune* in three separate years. He recorded the fastest time trial in history in 1994, when he completed the Lille prologue course at an average speed of 55.152 kph (34.270 mph), and he set the world hour record on three separate occasions.

Somewhat bizarrely, and quite appropriately given his propensity to eat them up, his middle name is Miles.

CHAPTER 6

CLASSIC RACING BIKES

*A winning bicycle brings together the expert of the
artisan, the latest in technological innovation, a passion
for the sport, and a fanatical attention to perfection.*

FAUSTO PINARELLO, ICONIC ITALIAN FRAME-BUILDER

Although racing bikes continue to have a saddle, two wheels and the
diamond-shaped frame they started with well over a hundred years
ago, their variations have in fact been many.

Raw materials have become lighter, with the progression from
heavy steel through to metal alloys like aluminium, to super-
lightweight carbon fibre, a polymer which has become so light that
the UCI has had to introduce a minimum weight for racing bikes (6.8
kg/15 lbs) in order to maintain a level playing field.

Aerodynamics have gone from not being given any thought
whatsoever to being one of the foremost considerations, especially
when it comes to the sleek time-trial bikes that are designed to shave
seconds that might ultimately result in Grand Tour or Olympic victory.

Rudimentary nineteenth-century single-gear bikes have
transmorphed into sophisticated twenty-first-century 20-gear
machines with electronic groupsets (the drivetrain of cogs and levers
and cables without which the bike will go nowhere).

Even individual components have somehow managed to become cool. Imagine what the nineteenth-century men of steel would have made of a Fizik Arione saddle made of manganese or a Speedplay Zero Nanogram pedal.

Bike designers and manufacturers have had to take all of these continually changing factors into account, but they have remained constant in one important respect – the loving care and attention that go into their products. Yesterday's bikes are today's classics, and today's bikes are exciting enough to be tomorrow's classics.

Let us look at just a few of the iconic bikes that have found their way into people's hearts and often into their rightful places in the record books:

Manufacturer: La Française
Model: Diamant (Diamond)
Released: c.1892
Frame: Steel

A robust-looking bike with wooden wheel rims on a much longer wheelbase than today's models, this is the monster that Maurice Garin rode to victory in the first-ever Tour de France in 1903. A single-speed bike with no freewheel, it wouldn't have been the easiest bike to take on a 2,428-km (1,517-mile) race, but Garin's sure looked the part, decked out in the red, white and blue of its French manufacturer.

Manufacturer: Bianchi
Model: Custom-built
Released: 1952
Frame: Steel

The classic of classics, this is the iconic celeste-green bike ridden by legendary Italian climber Fausto Coppi. On the back of his fourth Giro victory in 1952, Coppi rode the Bianchi to the first-ever, and first-televised, Tour de France summit finish at l'Alpe d'Huez. The components on his Bianchi that day included state-of-the-art aluminium handlebars supplied by Ambrosio and a Carnpagnolo Gran Sport derailleur.

Manufacturer: Lotus
Model: 108
Released: 1992
Frame: Carbon composite

This is the futuristic black-and-yellow time-trial bike that Chris Boardman used in the individual pursuit at the 1992 Barcelona Olympics to end Britain's 72-year wait for a cycling gold medal. The ultimate in aerodynamics at the time, as you might expect from a racing-car manufacturer, it had a full-disc rear wheel and a tri-spoke front wheel (both Mavic) mounted on a carbon-composite monocoque (that just means 'single-piece') frame. The handlebars shot out in the direction of travel in order to allow Boardman the aerodynamic 'skier's tuck' riding position.

Manufacturer: Graeme Obree
Model: 'Old Faithful'
Released: 1993
Frame: Steel

The Scottish rider Graeme Obree, a contemporary of Chris Boardman, rode the bike he had put together himself – which included parts from his own washing machine – to the world hour record in 1993. Obree was a pioneer of designs that allowed the skier's tuck and, once the UCI saw fit to ban that, the superman position (which the UCI also saw fit to ban). The 1993 record-breaking bike had tri-spoke Specialized carbon wheels and an innovative narrowing of the distance between the pedals. He dispensed with a top tube so that his close-together knees did not hit the frame. Obree also pedalled Old Faithful to the individual pursuit World Championship title in 1995.

Manufacturer: Specialized
Model: Venge
Released: 2011
Frame: Carbon

The American company that gave mountain bikes to the world in the 1980s spent the winter of 2010/11 in collaboration with McLaren of Formula One fame. Their joint venture was to provide a racing bike that was tailor-made for the fastest sprinter in the world, Britain's Mark Cavendish. Because Cavendish rides 'flat forward', with his nose over the front wheel, the design ensured that the front end was sufficiently strong and stiff for his unique riding style, while still incorporating the aerodynamics that you would expect McLaren to know a thing or two about. The collaboration worked, as this was the bike that Cavendish rode in 2011 to three Giro stages, five Tour stages and victory in the 2011 Road Race World Championships in Copenhagen.

Manufacturer: Cannondale
Model: Slice RS
Released: 2012
Frame: Carbon

US firm Cannondale's aluminium 'bad boy' bikes set tongues wagging in the traditional racing fraternity when they turned up in the late 1980s, looking more like mountain bikes than the slim, steel frames that the peloton was used to. But the feel of the bike and the flamboyance of Cannondale's biggest fan, the Italian rider Mario Cipollini, soon changed perception and the basic design became the forerunner of most of the racing bikes we see today. That pioneering has continued with the magnificently named Cannondale Slice RS time-trial and triathlon bike – the RS stands for 'rocket ship', and who wouldn't want a Cannondale Slice Rocket Ship? Everything is ultra-skinny, right down to the almost invisible seat post, and there isn't even a steer tube to pick up drag as you slice through time quicker than a Tardis.

Manufacturer: Pinarello
Model: Dogma 2
Released: 2012
Frame: Carbon

Pinarello enjoyed a golden period in the 1990s as Spaniard Miguel Indurain pedalled its bikes to five consecutive Tour de France victories and also cracked the world hour record on the Pinarello Blade specially designed for the purpose. The Dogma 2 later became the Sky Pro Cycling team's bike of choice, as used by Bradley Wiggins in becoming the first British winner of the Tour de France in 2012. Pinarello's latest models combine the strongest lightweight carbon yet devised with improved aerodynamics (for example, all cables are routed internally) and better balance (as further scientific testing continues to result in refinements to Pinarello's asymmetrical design).

Manufacturer: Pegoretti
Model: 'Big Leg Emma'
Released: 2003
Frame: Steel

A Dario Pegoretti frame can take up to two years to build and does not come cheap. His bikes are so sought-after that you are unlikely to find one on the second-hand market during your lifetime. Although he gives priority to the technical quality of the racing bike, he is revered in equal measure for his individualistic artistic design. He will use materials such as coffee grains or watercolour paints to achieve the detail or texture of the street art that inspires him, and his workshop is never devoid of the music that plays an equally big part in his inspirational work. As you may have guessed by now, one of his favourite tunes is the 1967 Frank Zappa single 'Big Leg Emma'.

CHAPTER 7

IN TRAINING

There is something wrong with a society that drives a car to a workout in the gym.

BILL NYE, AMERICAN SCIENCE EDUCATOR AND COMEDIAN
(POPULARLY KNOWN AS 'BILL NYE, THE SCIENCE GUY')

Many people cycle to keep fit and healthy, or in the hope of shedding a few pounds. If you are one of those people, you have chosen a remarkably clever option, because the bike absorbs a lot of the punishment your poor bones would have to take if you had chosen, say, running instead. On a bike, you get to enjoy the ride while simultaneously reaping the benefits of the exercise.

If, however, you want to cycle at a serious, even competitive, level, then you need to accept you are going to have to make your body suffer a bit in order to achieve your touring or racing goals. In which case, you might want to read up on the kind of training and nutrition that will help you achieve your ideal riding weight, which will bring you to the right amount of fitness at the right time and will aid your recovery from the rigours of long journeys or racing, or even from strain and injury.

You might look at photographs of the early cycling stars on the continent, with cigarettes hanging from their mouths and a hip flask of brandy in their back pockets, and conclude that all this modern sports science is really for wimps. But it's there, so you might as well use it.

Re-cycled Fact

Winter sun

Italy, Malta, Portugal, Cyprus and Spain, including the Canary Islands and Mallorca, are among the destinations that can provide you with warm-weather training camps if you need to escape the northern European cold and ice in winter. Sky Pro Cycling use Mallorca, so that obviously works.

Training regime

If you're a top professional rider, all you have to do is turn up and do as you're told whenever you're summoned to the team camp – complete with trainers, nutritionists, chefs and masseurs – and make sure you're not late for your session in the gym, altitude centre or wind tunnel.

If you're not, devise a training plan with the help of someone who understands the type of training you need for the kind of racing or touring you want to do. This might involve:

- Getting advice on your ideal riding/racing position

- Building up from low-intensity workouts in the gym

- A strength and conditioning programme to develop the core muscles that cycling alone can't reach

- Putting in the miles on the road to maximise your anaerobic capacity

- Maintaining a positive attitude, because the right frame of mind plus a strong injection of willpower will allow you to achieve more than you ever thought possible

- If you're getting serious, training at altitude – ride up and down mountains during the day but make sure you sleep at the top at night

- If you're getting really serious, finding a sports psychologist to tell you that you're unbeatable in heaven and on earth.

You might also consider creating your own indoor training regime. Simply purchase a 24-gear digital-console training bike with automatic tilt mechanism and use the software supplied to create your own 'authentic' routes in the French Alps or Canadian Rockies. Feel every incline and decline as if you were there and just the right amount of wind thanks to the 'intelligent wind resistance' you have factored in according to your own height, weight and riding-style profiles.

Nutrition

There is no shortage of books or online advice on healthy nutrition, or on the types of food and drink that are particularly suited to different types of exercise or training. You might also want to ascertain during your training sessions how your body reacts to which pre-race food and drink types (legal stimulants such as caffeine can offer a nice jolt if taken before a race, but not if you've discovered during training that it makes you jittery or anxious for a couple of hours), and which in-race foods and drinks give you the greatest boost.

Whatever your personal foibles and needs might be, you need to understand the basic fact that carbohydrates provide you with glucose, which you need to fuel your muscles, which you need to make your pedals turn (you probably knew that last bit anyway). Fats and proteins will also convert to glucose, but over a much longer period, and you'll probably have bonked by the time a Mars bar gets round to fuelling your muscles, so stick to carbs.

Because it's extremely difficult to eat a bowl of spaghetti bolognese during a race, however, you need to find other ways of taking on carbs. Dried fruit, sports drinks and energy bars are excellent choices, as are the energy gels that you see the top racers slugging at regular intervals.

So here is a handy summary of the golden rules to follow if you're racing or touring over long distances:

Eat before you're hungry   Take carbs every 30 minutes

Drink before you're thirsty

Golden rules on the go

Don't try to eat a bowl
of pasta on your bike
(especially not on a downhill
section of the race)

Always wash down your
carbs (especially energy
gels, which will otherwise
sit like gooey sludge in
the pit of your stomach)

Practise eating on your
bike beforehand (it's
very frustrating to keep
dropping it somewhere
between the back
pocket of your jersey
and your mouth).

Recovery foods

If you're at the serious end of the scale, you also need to understand the foodstuffs that will aid recovery from rigorous or long-term touring or riding, or from different types of injury. Proteins, vitamins, minerals and antioxidants help heal wounds, mend bones, and 'de-stress' tendons. Here are some examples:

- Carrots, spinach and sweet potatoes are good for 'road rash', as they contain vitamin A, which helps create the white blood cells essential for warding off the infection that can come from broken skin or flesh.

- Oranges, strawberries, peppers and broccoli will help repair tissues and cartilage by increasing collagen levels, an essential protein in the rebuilding of scar tissue, blood vessels and bone cells.

- Turkey, chicken, fish and sirloin steak are especially good for the concentrated protein that athletes need to recover quickly from injury – the last thing you want to do during the early stages of an injury, therefore, is reduce your protein intake because you think you need to compensate for a reduced level of exercise.

- Milk and yogurt contain the calcium that you need to repair injured muscle and bone, and also provide the vitamin D that improves calcium absorption, which in turn accelerates the repair process.

- Cereals provide the levels of zinc that are known to boost the immune system and heal wounds, and the carbohydrates that prevent your system from dipping into protein for energy, thereby leaving your protein free to undertake repairs.

- Salmon, tuna and trout are packed with the omega-3 fatty acids which quench inflammation, the natural enemy of recovery from tendonitis, bone fractures and sprained ligaments – anti-inflammatory drugs like ibuprofen can be surprisingly counterproductive in this respect, as they are said to overdo the quenching and you do apparently need some residual inflammation to aid the healing process.

Take it to the (VO₂) max

VO$_2$ may sound like shampoo to the uninitiated, but to the trained endurance athlete it means maximal oxygen consumption, or maximal aerobic capacity (V = volume, O$_2$ = oxygen and max = maximum). VO$_2$ max is reached when oxygen consumption remains at a steady rate notwithstanding an increased work rate, and can be expressed as millilitres of oxygen per kilogram of body weight per minute (ml/kg/min). To give you an idea of what this means in practical terms, consider the following (very rough) statistics, expressed as ml/kg/min, for average-sized people in their 'athletic prime':

Sedentary healthy female	35–40
Sedentary healthy male	40–45
Regular male cyclist	50–60
Professional male road racer	70–80
Top cross-country skier	80–90

There are plenty of exceptions to all of those very rough statistics, and the professional bike racers who have enjoyed the VO$_2$ levels of top cross-country skiers include five-times Tour de France winner Miguel Indurain of Spain (with a VO$_2$ of 88) and three-times Tour de France winner, American Greg LeMond (with a staggering 92.5). That aerobic capacity may have had something to do with them winning the Tour de France on multiple occasions!

And, finally, here are some rough statistics about the calories we are all so obsessed about burning in the twenty-first century (these ones are based on one hour of activity by a person weighing 59 kg (9 st 4 lb):

Playing the cello	118
Leisure cycling	136
Unicycling	295
Mountain biking	502
Road racing	708

So if mountain biking isn't your thing, try playing two cellos on a unicycle for an hour – it's pretty much the same thing in terms of staying fit and healthy.

CHAPTER 8

LOOKING THE PART

I'm not so sure about all the Lycra. I think the shorts and the pointy helmets they wear during the time trial are really odd.

PAUL SMITH, BRITISH FASHION DESIGNER

Cycling apparel has come a long way since the early days of woollen jerseys that weighed five times as much in the rain as they did in the sun, and the leather skid-lids that passed for helmets in continental Europe for much of the twentieth century. And women riders, no longer confined to the modest knickerbockers of yesteryear, have the same choices that men have.

As far as raw material was concerned, progress came in the way of the synthetics that were popularised in the second half of the twentieth century, like rayon and nylon and, for helmets, polystyrene. But even they seem antiquated in the face of today's water-repellent, mesh-ventilated, moisture-transferring, sun-protecting materials. In fact, clothing has become so sophisticated that different apparel and different levels of protection are available for different cycling sports. Take helmets: road racing demands a combination of lightweight materials and reinforced protection from concrete; mountain bikers require robust, secure-fitting headgear with thick chinstraps to absorb the bumps and jars of rocky terrain; and BMX riders need motorbike-style full-face helmets with chin bar and drop-down visor, and very little in the way of ventilation (because their races last an average of 40 seconds).

Re-cycled Fact

'Catch!'

When UCI road-racing rules made the wearing of helmets compulsory in 2003, an exception was made for final summit climbs of more than 5 km (3.1 miles) in length. This resulted in the bizarre spectacle in that year's Tour de France of rider after rider throwing their helmets in the general direction of team helpers on l'Alpe d'Huez.

To see just how far we've come in the twenty-first century, let's have a look at some of the state-of-the-art clothing items that road-racing pros wear nowadays on board their state-of-the-art bikes:

Helmet: Aerodynamic, lightweight and breathable, today's carbon-fibre helmets have come a long way from the leather skullcaps and polystyrene shells of yesteryear. The Kask Bambino TT (time-trial) helmet is a fine example of today's state-of-the-art design, being a sleek, black-and-white Buck-Rogers-style affair with integrated visor attached by magnets.

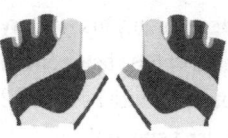

Gloves: Everything from superabsorbent to supergrip and superstretch to superventilated is available to the discerning pro rider, plus ergonomically positioned gel padding to distribute pressure evenly and absorb bumps, holes and cobbles.

Jersey: Fits like an extra layer of skin to reduce friction and ensure an aerodynamic ride; developed to keep heat out and control moisture.

Legwear: Cut for aggressive racing with scientifically designed padding. This is a very important clothing area for a rider, who is quite clearly never going to want his or her padding to be anything less than scientifically designed!

Time-trial skinsuit: Aerodynamic, wafer-thin, one-piece garment pre-tested in wind tunnels on the planet Jupiter. (I might have made up the bit about Jupiter, but you get my point.)

Shoes: Take the Bont Zero as an example: space-age design combined with space-age technology, these ergonomically shaped shoes weigh around 145 g (5 oz) each. Laminated silver glass-fibre uppers nestle on top of carbon monocoque soles. If Carlsberg designed cycling shoes…

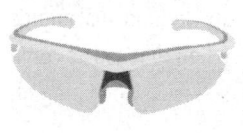

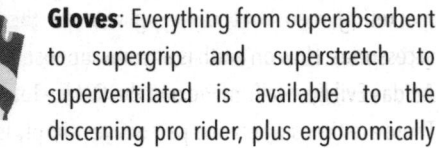

Eyewear: Lightweight, sweat-blocking, wraparound design and light-stabilising technology is matched only by the magnificence of the names that the marketing men have come up with for these twenty-first-century accessories. How on earth is anyone supposed to choose between the Adidas Evil Eye Halfrim Pro and the Oakley Tour de France RadarLock? There are times when one pair of eyes simply isn't enough!

Back on planet Earth, it is important to remember that perfectly ordinary clothing is fine for leisure-riding or short-distance commuting, providing that the clothing is not so loose fitting it could get caught up in a moving part. And never forget the option of pedal pushers, the most appropriately named item of clothing ever. Unless you live in a bike-friendly city like Amsterdam or Copenhagen, though, you might still want to consider a helmet if you're going into traffic.

If you do really want to look the part, you can spend several hundred pounds and beyond on top-of-the-range cycling gear from designer sportswear companies like Rapha. You can buy everything from base layers and arm warmers to wind jackets and African hair sheep leather gloves with military-level padding. Whether you consider this a bit unnecessary or not, you will be buying clothing that is likely to last you an awful lot of miles. You can also look out for special-edition clothing that commemorates this or that centenary, like the one hundredth running of the Tour de France in 2013, and keep an eye on the growing cycle-wear collection of keen cyclist and fashion icon Paul Smith.

In recent years, the top designers have added a new dimension to their collections, as it is now possible to buy 'city clothing' that affords you the same breathable, moisture-control cycling that you've come to expect on your daily commute, but which still looks good enough to wear all day in the workplace.

CHAPTER 9

FAMOUS EASY RIDERS

Nothing compares to the simple pleasure of a bike ride.
JOHN F. KENNEDY, 35TH PRESIDENT OF THE USA

This chapter looks at the myriad famous people who have fallen in love with the bicycle somewhere along the way, from writers and actors to pop stars, fashion designers and geniuses:

Entrepreneurs

Sir Paul Smith

British fashion designer Paul Smith dreamt of racing professionally until a serious accident on his bike at the age of 16 put paid to his ambitions. Professional cycling's loss turned out to be the fashion world's gain, although he has managed to combine his two passions whenever the opportunity has arisen. Working mostly with the sports designer Rapha, he has designed a range of cycle-wear, including a special-edition jersey to commemorate the visit of the Tour de France to British shores in 2007. He also worked with Derby bike manufacturer Mercian Cycles to design special-edition bikes that commemorated Mercian's sixtieth anniversary in 2006, and with Italian giant Pinarello to add a Paul Smith twist to their 2013 Dogma 65.1 Think 2 bikes.

Lord Alan Sugar

The British entrepreneur, and godfather of *The Apprentice*, took to cycling after a series of injuries forced him to give up his first sporting love, tennis. Sir Alan regularly completes a 50-mile loop around the Essex countryside on his top-of-the-range Pinarello racing bike.

Other famous bike-riding entrepreneurs include:

- Vivienne Westwood (extrovert English fashion designer, who commutes to work on her Pashley).
- Richard Branson (the Virgin boss has completed the 109.5-km – 68-mile – Cape Argus tour in South Africa – see also Matt Damon below).
- Clive Sinclair (developer of the doomed C5 car and the lightweight A-bike, which folds down small enough to fit into a rucksack).

🎵 Musicians

John Lennon

'I must have been the happiest boy in Liverpool, if not the world,' John Lennon said of the time he was given his first bike after passing his 11-plus exam. It was a Raleigh Lenton Mk II and he loved it so much that he took it to bed with him that night. In later years he was often photographed riding a bike, including with his fellow Beatles and with Yoko Ono. He even had a white bike to ride around the inside of the Hilton Hotel in Amsterdam when he was on honeymoon there with Yoko.

Eric Clapton

Music aficionados may be familiar with the *Disraeli Gears* album that propelled the British band Cream (consisting of Eric Clapton, Ginger Baker and Jack Bruce) to 'supergroup' status in the late 1960s. Not all will be aware that the album title derived from a cycling malapropism. Eric Clapton was a former bike racer who had been forced to choose between the bike and the guitar, at least as far as his career was concerned. He was talking in the recording studio one day about the new racing bike he was thinking of buying when somebody asked him whether it had 'Disraeli gears' (meaning, of course, 'derailleur gears'). The album title was decided there and then.

Madonna

The American pop superstar, actress and film director is often seen riding around London, New York and Malibu (i.e. near whichever home she happens to be staying in at the time). She uses her bike to get to the gym or the recording studio as part of her overall fitness regime.

David Byrne

The Scottish former Talking Heads front man does not own a car and is an active supporter of cycling, having used it as his main form of transport for most of his life, especially in his adopted city of New York. He has a regular cycling column in the *New York Times* and has written more widely on the subject also, including a 2009 book called *Bicycle Diaries*.

In 2008 he designed a series of bicycle parking racks in the style of the area they were to be placed in – such as a dollar sign for Wall Street and a coffee mug on Amsterdam Avenue near the Hungarian Pastry Shop.

Other famous bike-riding musicians include:

- Beyoncé Knowles (iconic American singer/songwriter/dancer/actress who says she rides to keep herself grounded).
- Ian Brown (English singer/songwriter and front man with 1990s indie band The Stone Roses – rode his bike slowly through the streets of London's Soho and Chinatown for the video for his solo single 'F.E.A.R.', which was then reversed to create the impression of him riding slowly backwards).
- Tim Commerford (bass player with American rock band Rage Against The Machine – they had to cancel a concert in 1995 after Commerford broke his wrist in a cycling accident).
- Lily Allen (English singer/songwriter who gave the Raleigh Chopper something of a comeback in the 2006 video for her 'LDN' single).
- Sting (English musician and singer/songwriter, and front man with The Police – can be seen riding around his Tuscan vineyard estate with wife Trudie Styler).

 *Actors*

Matt Damon

The American Hollywood actor is a keen cyclist and has completed the 109.5-km (68-mile) Cape Argus event in South Africa on a tandem with his brother Kyle (the Cape Argus attracts more riders than any other sportive on the planet – around 35,000 riders took part in 2013). Damon was due to play Lance Armstrong in a film adaption of Armstrong's biography *It's Not About the Bike*, but that probably doesn't sound like such a good career move since Armstrong lost his superhero status.

Other famous bike-riding actors include:

- Brad Pitt (American actor and film producer – often 'papped' cycling *en famille* around LA).
- Angelina Jolie (American actress and UN Special Envoy for Refugees – see Brad Pitt).
- Hugh Jackman (Australian actor and producer, who had the wheels stolen from his bike during his audition for *Les Misérables* – at least he got the part).
- Gwyneth Paltrow (American actress, singer and food writer; also married to a unicyclist – see Chris Martin, below).
- Pierce Brosnan (Irish actor, film producer and environmentalist with a licence to ride).
- Jennifer Aniston (American actress who worked as a bike messenger before hitting the big time as Rachel in *Friends*).

Re-cycled Fact

Tri-actors

Harrison Ford, Jennifer Lopez and Jon Hamm (of Mad Men fame), have all been known to compete in triathlons, which has no doubt helped them to look so good over the years. The image seems well suited to the Indiana Jones character, and to J-Lo's booty-shaking routines, but not so much to the chain-smoking, whisky-drinking, womanising Don Draper. Never judge a 1950s ad-man by his cover.

TV presenters

Jeremy Clarkson

The TV presenter gets the award for Biggest Hypocrite on Two Wheels. Notwithstanding his public rants about the need to ban cyclists because they obstruct his beloved cars and don't even pay road tax, he has often been seen at weekends enjoying sneaky cycling trips with his wife.

Other famous bike-riding TV presenters (all of whom support the cycling cause and do much to raise money for charities with bike-related events) include:

- Lorraine Kelly (Scottish breakfast TV anchorwoman and cycling ambassador).
- David Walliams (English comedian, writer and actor – completed a John O'Groats to Land's End [JOGLE] charity run in 2010 in spite of a serious fall in the Lake District).
- Phil Keoghan (New Zealand-born TV presenter of American travel game show *The Amazing Race*).
- Mike Tomalaris (Australian TV's 'Mr Cycling' – has covered the Tour de France since 1996).
- Ryan van Duzer (US TV presenter who has cycled across America and from Honduras to Colorado).
- Patrick Kielty (Northern Irish comedian and TV presenter, a member of David Walliams's JOGLE team in 2010).
- Fearne Cotton (English TV and radio presenter, and another 2010 JOGLER).

 *Scientists*

Albert Einstein

When he wasn't being a genius, Einstein often relaxed by riding around on his bike. Even then, he didn't totally switch off, though, because he once said that he thought of the theory of relativity while out riding. He also compared life with riding a bike, saying that 'to keep your balance, you must keep moving'. As if we didn't already know that – it's not exactly rocket science, is it, Albert?

Other famous bike-riding scientists include:

- David Attenborough (English broadcaster and second-to-none naturalist, who cycles whenever he can).

Writers

Mark Twain

Mark Twain learnt to ride on a penny-farthing in the early 1880s. It did not come easily to him, and he penned a typically hilarious account of the experience in his essay *Taming the Bicycle*. In this, he describes how he managed to hospitalise his instructor by constantly landing on top of him, and how he managed to perfect the 'voluntary dismount', but only long after he had perfected the involuntary version. He concludes the essay with the following advice to his readers: 'Get a bicycle. You will not regret it, if you live.'

Other famous bike-riding writers include:

- Arthur Conan Doyle (English author of the Sherlock Holmes stories, including the 1903 short story *The Adventure of the Solitary Cyclist*).
- Ernest Hemingway (American writer and journalist; a keen cyclist and an avid follower of European road racing between the world wars).
- Leo Tolstoy (Russian writer who learned to ride at the age of 67).
- Thomas Hardy (English novelist and poet, who loved to ride to avoid contact with other human beings).
- Sylvia Plath (American novelist and poet, who imported her own bike when she went to study at Cambridge in the 1950s).
- H.G. Wells (English writer who indulged his love of cycling in an 1896 novel about a cycling holiday, *The Wheels of Chance*).
- Philip Larkin (bald, bespectacled and bicycle-clipped English poet and novelist who loved to visit churches on his bike).
- Virginia Woolf (English writer who travelled far and wide across the Sussex countryside as a teenager by combining rail and bicycle travel).

Sportsmen and women

Jensen Button

Cycling forms an integral part of the English Formula One driver's training regime. He tests his fitness on the infamous 12-km (7.5-mile) Col de la Madone ('Madonna climb') near Menton on the French Riviera, and therefore not far from his home in Monte Carlo.

Zara Phillips

The top equestrian and granddaughter of Queen Elizabeth II may be more comfortable on a horse, but she has proved pretty handy on a bike as well on the occasions she has turned out to play bicycle polo for charity.

Lawrence Dallaglio and Freddie Flintoff

The English rugby and cricket sporting legends raised over £2 million for charity when they spearheaded a team of 15 riders across an epic 2,782-km challenge over 22 days from Olympia in Greece (the home of the Olympics) to London in 2012.

Other famous bike-riding sportsmen and women include:

- David Beckham (former England footballer who won league titles in four different countries – has often been snapped out riding with his sons in LA).
- Tiger Woods (American golfing superstar, who starts most days with a run or a bike ride as part of his strict physical training regime).
- Fernando Alonso (Spanish Formula One driver who rides his bike at close to professional pace).
- Abby Wambach (top American women's soccer player who loves to mountain bike).
- Sir Geoff Hurst (English hat-trick hero of the 1966 World Cup football final, who still rides for charitable causes).

👑 Politicians and royals

Boris Johnson

London's high-profile cycling mayor continues to push for more, safer cycling lanes in the UK's capital. He famously scrapped the 'bendy buses' because of concerns that cyclists might get trapped on the inside as the buses negotiated their way around corners.

Crown Prince Frederik and Crown Princess Mary of Denmark

The Crown Prince and his Australian-born wife cycle regularly in and around the palace grounds and think nothing of ferrying their young children to school in a cargo bike.

Other famous bike-riding politicians and royals include:

- John F. Kennedy (35th president of the USA).
- Barack Obama (44th president of the USA – often photographed out riding with his family or with celebrity 'mates' like Brad Pitt).
- Queen Beatrix of the Netherlands (there is even a life-size bronze statue of her riding her bike, but she will have more time for the real thing in any event since she abdicated the throne in 2013).
- David Cameron (British prime minister, who famously had his bike stolen while he picked up a few bits of salad in his local Tesco in west London).
- Arnold Schwarzenegger (Austrian-American actor and former governor of California, often snapped riding 'stateside' and took to the London streets on a Barclays 'Boris' bike in 2012 with the London mayor himself).

Famous unicyclists

Chris Martin

If evidence were required that the Coldplay singer/songwriter and instrumentalist could ride a unicycle, it can be found in the band's video for their 2011 'Paradise' single, when he unicycled on the South African plains in an elephant costume (as you do).

Mark Owen, Jason Orange and Howard Donald

The Take That members learnt to unicycle for their 2009 *The Circus* tour, bringing the house down whenever they unicycled on to the stage, only to be trumped by Gary Barlow following behind on a miniature clown's bike.

Eddie Izzard

As he proved in a 2008 episode of hit Channel 4 show *TFI Friday*, the British comedian and actor Eddie Izzard can do more than just unicycle - he can escape from the 'Manacles of Death' within 10 seconds while riding a unicycle!

Michael Crawford

The English actor/singer learned to unicycle, juggle, walk a tightrope, trampoline and walk on stilts for his lead role in the 1980s hit stage musical *Barnum*, based on the life of the eponymous circus showman.

Other famous unicyclists include:

- Rupert Grint (English actor who played Ron Weasley in *Harry Potter*).
- Mika Häkkinen (Finnish former Formula One racing driver).
- Donald Rumsfeld (former US Secretary of Defense).

BIGGER, BETTER, FASTER, STRANGER...

A bicycle ride around the world begins with a single pedal stroke.
SCOTT STOLL, AMERICAN ROUND-THE-WORLD CYCLIST

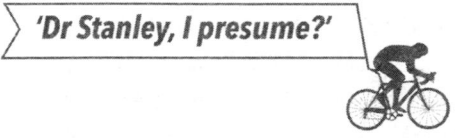

'Dr Stanley, I presume?'

British-American Tom Stevens was the first person to circle the globe by bicycle, and he did so on a penny-farthing between April 1884 and December 1886. He started off by crossing the plains and mountains of America from San Francisco to Boston, astonishing cowboys and Indians alike as he went.

Having sailed east to Liverpool, he cycled through Berkhamsted, the town of his birth, before taking the Newhaven-Dieppe ferry to continental Europe. He later rested in Constantinople before taking in Mesopotamia (present-day Iraq) and Persia (present-day Iran), where he saw out a winter as a guest of the Shah. Afghanistan, India, China and Japan followed.

A couple of years following his circumnavigation, this remarkable man led a successful East African expedition to find Henry Morton Stanley, the explorer who had found David Livingstone and then wandered 'off map' himself. Between them, they must have had some stories to tell around the campfire.

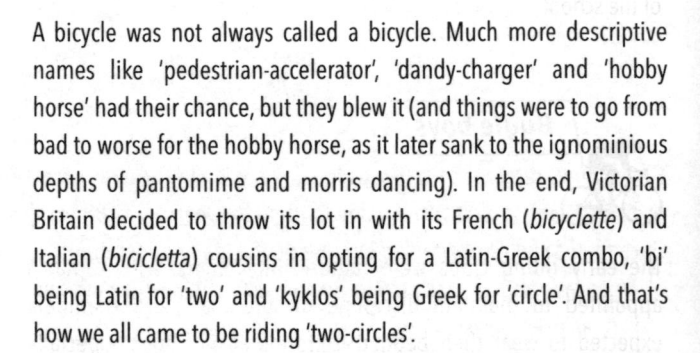

What's in a name?

A bicycle was not always called a bicycle. Much more descriptive names like 'pedestrian-accelerator', 'dandy-charger' and 'hobby horse' had their chance, but they blew it (and things were to go from bad to worse for the hobby horse, as it later sank to the ignominious depths of pantomime and morris dancing). In the end, Victorian Britain decided to throw its lot in with its French (*bicyclette*) and Italian (*bicicletta*) cousins in opting for a Latin-Greek combo, 'bi' being Latin for 'two' and 'kyklos' being Greek for 'circle'. And that's how we all came to be riding 'two-circles'.

Tread carefully, my dear Watson

Arthur Conan Doyle was a keen solo cyclist and was also photographed on a high-wheel tandem tricycle with Mrs Doyle (probably his first wife, Louisa). It was only natural, then, that he should imbue Sherlock Holmes with superlative bicycle-tread-spotting abilities. As Sherlock declared in *The Adventure of the Priory School*, 'I am familiar with 42 different impressions left by tyres.' On the particular tyre impression in question, he further explained to a confused Watson: 'This track, as you perceive, was made by a rider who was going from the direction of the school.'

Bugle boys

The early riding clubs were rather stuffy affairs, with captains appointed to maintain discipline on the road, and members expected to wear their badged uniforms at all times, especially when out riding. Potholes were the natural enemy of the penny-farthing in particular, and so each club had a bugle boy up front to sound the alarm whenever he came across a hole or rut (which was often).

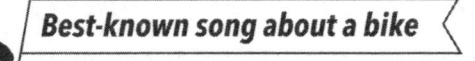

Best-known song about a bike

Mungo Jerry ('Push Bike Song'), Hawkwind ('Silver Machine') and Katie Melua ('Nine Million Bicycles') are strong contenders for Best-known Bike Song, but the award must surely go to 'Bicycle Race', from Queen's 1978 *Fat Bottomed Girls* album. Altogether now: 'I want to ride my bicycle…'

Most painful joke about a bike

*Truth hurts. Maybe not as much as jumping on a
bicycle with the seat missing, but it hurts.*
LIEUTENANT FRANK DREBIN (LESLIE NIELSEN),
THE NAKED GUN 2 1/2: THE SMELL OF FEAR

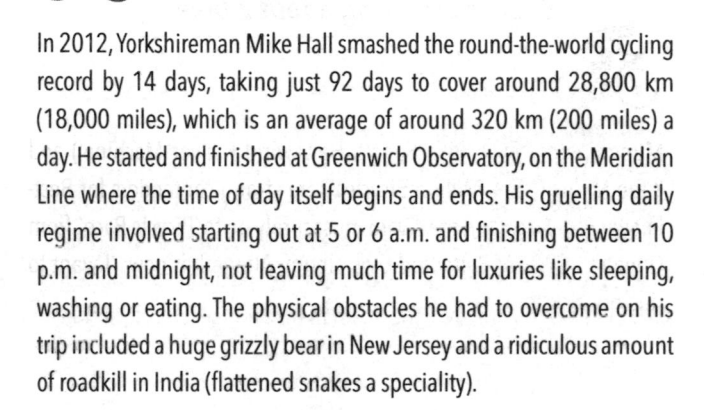

The beginning and end of time

In 2012, Yorkshireman Mike Hall smashed the round-the-world cycling record by 14 days, taking just 92 days to cover around 28,800 km (18,000 miles), which is an average of around 320 km (200 miles) a day. He started and finished at Greenwich Observatory, on the Meridian Line where the time of day itself begins and ends. His gruelling daily regime involved starting out at 5 or 6 a.m. and finishing between 10 p.m. and midnight, not leaving much time for luxuries like sleeping, washing or eating. The physical obstacles he had to overcome on his trip included a huge grizzly bear in New Jersey and a ridiculous amount of roadkill in India (flattened snakes a speciality).

The BT Million Pound Bike Ride

In 2010 seven celebrities raised over £1 million for the Sport Relief charity when they cycled in shifts from John O'Groats to Land's End in four days. TV presenters Davina McCall and Fearne Cotton joined comedians David Walliams, Jimmy Carr, Miranda Hart, Russell Howard and Patrick Kielty to endure sub-zero temperatures, blizzards, cuts, bruises and saddle sores to achieve their mission. I hope someone had the decency to run them a nice, hot bath when they got to the finish.

Count Learner Tolstoy

As we have seen, the many great writers who have used bike-riding as a form of relaxation away from the writing desk include Ernest Hemingway, Thomas Hardy, Sylvia Plath, H.G. Wells, Philip Larkin, Virginia Woolf, Leo Tolstoy and Arthur Conan Doyle. None of the others, however, was as old as Leo Tolstoy when they learnt to ride. Tolstoy was 67 when, in 1895, the Moscow Society of Velocipede-Lovers provided him with a free bike and instruction, in the hope that it would help him get over the death of his youngest (13th) child.

The art of cycling

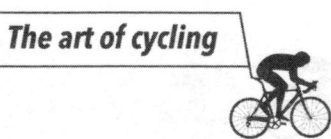

Salvador Dalí's affection for cycling is reflected in a number of his paintings, in some of which a horde of bearded cyclists ride in various directions with different objects on their heads: round stones in *Illumined Pleasures* (1929); long loaves of bread in *Babaouo* (1932); and heavy stones that hold down the ends of a wedding veil as the bikes are ridden by deathly figures past a grand piano in *Sentimental Conversation* (1944).

Droopy chaps and frisky gals

Saddles have always been a cause for concern for people who ride bikes for long periods, and were a particular concern for those early riders who cycled over potholes, ruts and cobblestones. The threat to male sexual performance and productivity was seen as very real, and resulted in the trial of many different saddle sizes and materials. It also spawned the groin-protecting 'bike jockey strap', or 'jockstrap'.

Victorian society quickly concluded that the problem for women, however, was quite the opposite of impotence, and manufacturers sought solutions to the otherwise inevitable state of permanent arousal in the female bike rider. Saddles were split in two to ensure that ladies rested on their sitting bones as opposed to their, er, non-sitting bones.

A little corner of Italy

Cycling is popular in many African countries owing to the influence of their one-time Italian and French colonial rulers. This is especially true in the former Italian colony of Eritrea, in East Africa, where road cycling is the national sport and rider Daniel Teklehaymanot has reigned supreme as African national champion for over three years. In the capital, Asmara, there are said to be more pizzerias, ice-cream parlours and cappuccino-serving coffee bars per square metre than anywhere else outside of Italy.

Most southerly bike ride

Thomas Orde-Lees was a member of Ernest Shackleton's 1914–1917 Trans-Antarctic Expedition. A fitness fanatic, he took his bike with him and took every opportunity to ride it on the pack ice whenever the *Endurance* got stuck (which was often).

Most people on a bike ride

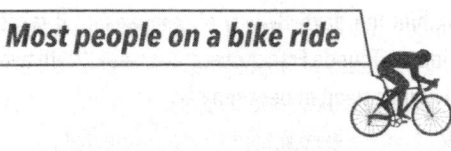

On New Year's Eve 2011, tens of thousands of Taiwanese took to their bikes simultaneously to establish a world record for the number of participants in a mass bike ride. One local news source put the figure at 72,919; another put it at 114,606. Either way, it was an appropriate record for a country that houses Giant, the largest bike-manufacturing company in the world.

Most banned substances

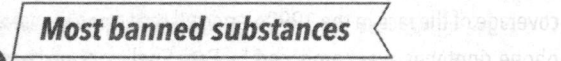

In 2012, French amateur rider Alexandre Dougnier was banned after a urine sample revealed a total of 12 banned substances, thought to be a record for a single sample.

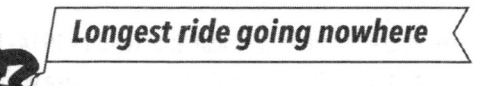

Longest ride going nowhere

In 2010, 52-year-old American George Hood set the world record for the longest time riding a stationary bike: 222 hours, 22 minutes, 22 seconds. As he was allowed a five-minute break for every hour he was in the saddle, it took him ten days. By way of comparison, it takes around 92 hours to ride the Tour de France over three weeks, with two rest days and a good night's sleep in between stages.

Never Mind the Buzzcocks

The Tour de France theme tune made popular by Channel 4's coverage of the race in the 1990s, and still the sound of many mobile phone ringtones, was composed by Pete Shelley of punk rock band Buzzcocks fame.

Guinness World Records

The official Guinness World Records lists 52 results in the cycling category. Here are my top ten:

1. Farthest distance cycled in a year (120,805 km/75,065 miles) – by Englishman Tommy Godwin in 1939.

2. World hour record (49.441 km/30.9 miles) – by Englishman Chris Boardman at Manchester Velodrome in 2000, beating Eddy Merckx's previous record by 10 metres.

3. Longest distance cycling backwards on a unicycle (109.4 km/68 miles) – by American Steve Gordon in 1999.

4. Highest bunny hop over a static bar on a bicycle (1.42 metres/4 ft 8 in) – by Spaniard Benito Ros in 2009.

5. Fastest downhill speed on a bicycle on snow or ice (222 km/h/138 mph) – by Frenchman Eric Barone at Les Arcs in 2000.

6. Farthest distance cycled underwater (3.04 km/1.87 miles, in 3 hours, 35 minutes, 23 seconds) – by American Ashrita Furman in an Olympic swimming pool in Coimbra, Portugal, in 2011.

7. Longest distance cycled in one hour with no hands (37.4 km/23.25 miles) – by American Erik Skramstad over 62 laps of the Las Vegas Speedway track in 2009.

8. Most vertical metres cycled in 24 hours (20,049.9 metres) – achieved simultaneously by Austrian twins Horst and Gernot Turnowsky in the Austrian Alps in 2007.

9. First trick cycling 'loop the loop' (1904) – by an Ancillotti troupe member at the Barnum Bailey Circus.

10. Most consecutive artistic cycling rounds In the raiser head tube reverse/ shoulderstand position (four) – by German sisters Carla and Henriette Hochdorfer in 2010. I don't know what this means but it sounds mighty impressive!

Annie 'Londonderry'

Latvian-born American Annie Kopchovsky was the first woman to cycle round the world, travelling only with a change of clothing and a pearl-handled revolver. The Londonderry Lithia Spring Water Company paid her to carry its placard on her bike and to adopt their name as her own. Setting off alone from Boston in 1894, at the age of 24 and already a mother of three children, she took nine months to cycle through parts of France, Egypt, Jerusalem, modern-day Yemen, Sri Lanka and Singapore. Arriving back in San Francisco, she took another six months to cycle the length and breadth of America before finally returning to Boston.

Doggone!

Dogs were more than just a nuisance to the early cyclists, especially those cyclists who were atop high-wheelers like the penny-farthing, who could easily be toppled by the wee, jumping, barking beasts. Victorian cyclists carried small-calibre pistols to take care of the problem (remember, this was back in the days before dogs were afforded the same status in society as human children); American riders carried ammonia sprays; and German riders went the whole hog with gunpowder-filled anti-dog grenades.

Can't beat the real thing...

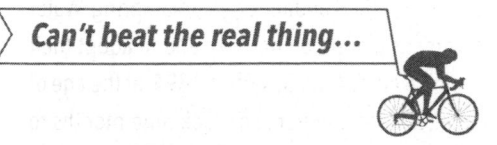

The Uzbek sprinter Djamolidine Abdoujaparov terrified TV commentators with his nine syllables and fellow riders with his erratic, flailing riding style. Things came to a head in 1991, on the final Tour de France stage sprint on the Champs-Elysées, when the 'Tashkent Terror', as he was unaffectionately known, swerved into an oversized cardboard 'coke can' on the barriers and came off his bike with sufficient force to break his collarbone, on top of numerous other minor injuries and concussion. Because he was taken to hospital, he is the only winner of the Tour's green jersey competition to miss the presentation of his own prize on the Champs-Elysées (he had eventually limped over the line before being taken to hospital, as it was a requirement to finish the race in order to win the competition).

Daredevil rider

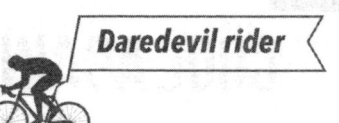

The most famous of all the Niagara daredevils, 'The Great Blondin' (real name, Jean François Gravelet) crossed Niagara Falls on a tightrope several times in the second half of the nineteenth century. On one occasion, he delighted the watching crowds by doing so on a bicycle. On other occasions he walked it blindfold, or on stilts, or pushing a wheelbarrow, or with his manager on his back.

Extreme biking

Extreme biking has taken many forms, from cycling along shark-infested seabeds to riding out to the edge of a precipice over the Grand Canyon; from leaping gorges to riding along unprotected cliff edges; from freefall parachuting (with your bike to break the landing) to frightening downhill descents like the infamous Repack in Fairfax, California. I have set a target of how many of those amazing feats I would like to achieve in my lifetime. None.

CHAPTER 11

COOL AGAIN!

I hope you have enjoyed my miscellaneous ramblings about all things bike and that you feel inspired to do more of whatever it is you want to do on whatever size and shape of bike that is suited to your needs.

The great news for us all is that, after the ups and downs of the past hundred years or so, cycling has done more than just survive into the twenty-first century – it has begun to flourish all over again. The sport of road racing in particular has gone global. Bike technology continues to develop at an impressive pace, and sales of bikes are on a distinctly upward trend. The cycling infrastructure in town and country is improving all the time. It has taken a while, but cycling has without doubt become cool again.

So enjoy being cool. It doesn't matter how you ride, just ride. Do it for fun, to stay fit and healthy, to clear your head, to feed your need for speed or to satisfy your competitive urges. Or all of the above.

I leave you with the profound words of the great Eddy Merckx when asked what advice he might give to other riders:

Ride lots.

mud
sweat&
GEARS

CYCLING FROM LAND'S END TO
JOHN O'GROATS (VIA THE PUB)

JOHN O'GROATS

LAND'S END

ellie bennett

Mud, Sweat and Gears
Cycling from Land's End to John o'Groats
(Via the Pub)

Ellie Bennett

ISBN: 978 1 84953 220 4   Paperback   £8.99

As Ellie's fiftieth birthday approaches and her ambitions of a steady income, a successful career and an ascent of Everest seem as far away as ever, she begins to doubt she's capable of achieving anything at all. So when her best friend Mick suggests a gruelling cycle ride from Land's End to John o'Groats, she takes up the challenge.

They opt for the scenic route which takes them along cycle paths, towpaths and the back roads and byways of Britain, unable to resist sampling local beers in the pubs they pass along the way. But as the pints start to stack up faster than the miles they're putting under their tyres, Ellie wonders if they'll ever make it to the finishing line…

'Ellie Bennett is funny, she can talk the rear wheel off a Dawes three-speed and she loves a decent pint. I'd tag along with her any day'

OZ CLARKE

'great fun and surprisingly informative'

MARK BEAUMONT, AUTHOR OF *THE MAN WHO CYCLED THE WORLD*

'Ellie Bennett takes on the End-to-End with plentiful supplies of humour and beer'

JOSIE DEW

If you're interested in finding out more about our books,
find us on Facebook at **Summersdale Publishers** and follow us
on Twitter at **@Summersdale**.

www.summersdale.com